ENTERPRISE VALUE

HOW THE BEST OWNER-MANAGERS BUILD
THEIR FORTUNE, CAPTURE THEIR COMPANY'S
GAINS, AND CREATE THEIR LEGACY

PETER R. WORRELL

New York   Chicago   San Francisco   Athens   London
Madrid   Mexico City   Milan   New Delhi
Singapore   Sydney   Toronto

2 3 4 5 6 7 8 9 0   QFR/QFR 0 9 8 7 6 5 4

ISBN 978-0-07-181788-2
MHID 0-07-181788-3

e-ISBN 978-0-07-181789-9
e-MHID 0-07-181789-1

Library of Congress Cataloging-in-Publication Data

Worrell, Peter R.
  Enterprise value: how the best owner-managers build their fortune, capture their company's gains, and create their legacy / Peter R. Worrell.
    pages cm
  ISBN 978-0-07-181788-2 (hardback)—ISBN 0-07-181788-3 (hardback)
1. Entrepreneurship. 2. Management. I. Title.
  HB615.W684 2013
  658.4'21—dc23
                                                              2013020009

McGraw-Hill Education books are available at special quantity discounts to use as premiums and sales promotions or for use in corporate training programs. To contact a representative, please visit the Contact Us pages at www.mhprofessional.com.

To Bigelow's Entrepreneur Owner-Manager Clients—the ones we know well and to the ones we have not yet met—this book is dedicated to you. You are the greatest teachers in the world.

Author's Note

ALL OF THE STORIES IN THIS BOOK ARE BASED ON ACTUAL engagements and relationships that my firm and I have had with our clients and friends over the years. All of the names, industries, locations, and other details have been changed to ensure the confidentiality and privacy of the people and companies involved. None of the stories are composites.

One hundred percent of the profits from the sale of this book will fund scholarships to increase access to not-for-profit higher education.

Contents

Acknowledgments

THIS BOOK ORIGINATED BECAUSE I FELT "CALLED" TO WRITE IT TO answer the observations from many of my friends and clients after they successfully completed a wealth creation transaction: "Dammit, Pete, if I had only known then what I know now."

If we at Bigelow have in some way moved toward that goal of knowing, then much of the credit goes to several sets of positive individuals who contributed in various ways to this work. I want to gratefully acknowledge them.

My obligation and gratitude for many people's influence at the intersection of my professional and personal learning is wide, and their constant inspiration pervades this whole book. Since July 1, 1980, my professional home has been at Bigelow. This work is a result of close collaboration of minds during that time with the entire Bigelow team. While I have taken the lead in this work, to the greatest possible extent this book is the result of our collective experiences where many of my Bigelow teammates played a starring role. All of Bigelow's clients have informed this work, but especially a group that includes Jack Weeks, Walter Salter, David Williams, Steve Watson, Eric Frey, David Stuebe, Bill Dunlap, Chris Pierce, David Gould, Bill Gundy, Keith Shaughnessy, Stuart Mathews, Marty Elkin, Charlie Malachias, Marilyn Moss, Peter Duffield, Art Cleary, Bruce Olsen, Bob Horgan, Irwin Muskat, Lin Galeucia, Peter Getman, Barrett McDevitt, Michael Desrosiers, Jackie Russ,

Jeff Webster, John Webster, Scott Webster, Kevin Schinze, Michael McGrath, George Burrill, George Chandler, Reed Hampden, Andrew Schonbek, Phil Goldman, Paul Amato, John Harvey, Fred Gunzner, Frank Singer, Chris Papoutsy, Harry Indursky, John Powell, Gene Slusser, Ed Stevens, Eli Manchester, Jim Cooper, Jeff Lamm, Andy Stickney, Hod Irvine, Jim Tyrie, Don Farris, Bob Derecktor, Carl Boll, Charlie Stinson, Dexter Stowell, Jim Levis, Mike Foster, David Cohen, Bob Smith, Howard Nichols, Nelson Gifford, George Psyhojos, Bill Stone, Jack Jensen, Jim Stein-Sharpe, Debbie Stein-Sharpe, David MacMahon, Roland Sutton, Todd Baldree, Buddy Long, Ben Holbrook, Ted Cronin, Susie Cronin, Bill Early, Dave Moreland, David Adams, Bill McCourt, David McCourt, Michael Ross, Ford Reiche, Claire Parker, Brad Parker, Bill Findeisen, Tom Shaffner, Bill Purington, Ted Purington, Pat Robins, Larry Sudbay, Nicole Carignan, Jack Brewer, Rives Potts, Andy Barowsky, Albert Lepage, John McDonough, Jeff Diggins, Dave Slutz, and Barry Hibble.

Richard Kimball, who was an early mentor, believed in me and is still patient with me. Phil Ryan's clever stories and Ferd Ensinger's "parables" continue to inform Bigelow lore. David Linton and Rob MacLeod are my partners at Bigelow and are two of my closest friends as well; no one could hope for or even dream of having more completely energizing, effective, and supportive partners than I have in Rob and David. Derek Stern's thoughtful reading of early manuscripts and overall guidance has been like a gyroscope—some critical, some not, but always balanced. All of these people provided incredibly insightful feedback.

I have been the beneficiary of many great teachers and serious academic professionals steeped in their specialized fields who provided a lot of the important theoretical foundation I have been applying to entrepreneur owner-managers and which is reflected in this book.

They include Marian Marchand, John Carvellas, Vince Bolduc, Don Sutton, Marc vanderHeyden, Chris Peterson, David Cooperrider, Angela Duckworth, and especially Marty Seligman.

Several people whose input I value read and many generously commented on early drafts or partial drafts of this work, for which I am very grateful, including Marty Seligman, Angela Duckworth, Bill Sahlman, Barry Schwartz, Richard Zeckhauser, Paul LeBlanc, Bill Achtmeyer, Patty Stonesifer, Les Charm, Ford Reiche, Marisa Lister, Rena Janus, Kim Goodman, Greg Perry, John-Michael Girald, Denise Burke, Stephen McGee, Warren Widener, Lissa Gumprecht, and Sarah Pendleton.

This book has greatly benefited from my close collaboration with John Butman and his colleague Anna Weiss at Idea Platforms, Inc. John, after receiving what I thought was a nearly complete manuscript, was unafraid to (metaphorically speaking) stuff it in a Cuisinart and flick the switch. When I became anxious about that, he patiently summarized some of the logical and other challenges in the manuscript and most of all gave the Solomonic advice (many times): remain calm. And with his extremely professional help in disassembling, reassembling, and editing, I did so (or tried to). Thank you, John.

I was introduced to John Butman through my literary agents, Ike Williams and Carol Franco at Kneerim & Williams. After reading very early drafts both Ike and Carol were very encouraging, suggesting thematic changes and title changes, giving me needed momentum, and ultimately introducing me to my friend Tom Miller, executive editor at my publisher, McGraw-Hill. Tom and McGraw-Hill's utter professionalism have earned my admiration many times over. Thank you, Tom.

Ike Williams was introduced to me by Bryn Zeckhauser. From our first conversation, Bryn was extremely enthusiastic and encouraging. When early on I tentatively answered her question about who my literary agent was by telling her I was leaning to self-publishing, she had the intellectual weight and sense of humor that made her opinion very clear in the "Are you kidding me?" answer. Thank you, Bryn.

My parents, Bob and Loraine Worrell, both interested and prolific readers as well as parents, provided great support and positive reinforcement at all times. But without a doubt, my ultimate appreciation naturally goes to my wife and life companion, Dr. Kareen K. Worrell, who, from the beginning, realized, accepted, and supported the notion that her husband is passionately committed both to her and to his work.

Introduction: What Happens at the End?

> If you treat an individual as he is, he will stay as he is,
> but if you will treat him as if he were what he
> ought to be and could be, then he will become
> what he ought to be and could be.
>
> —GOETHE

LET'S BEGIN WITH AN ENDING.

One April afternoon in 2010, at about 3:30, the executive vice president of Material Tech called all three hundred employees of that company to the cafeteria for a special announcement. At Material Tech, a high-tech manufacturer of precision parts made from exotic alloys for the medical and energy industries, this was an unusual occurrence. So everybody hurried out of his or her office and left stations on the manufacturing plant floor. The employees speculated about what was going on and seated themselves at the tables and on folding chairs. The cold room, with a gray linoleum floor and vending machines lined up along one wall, became overcrowded with two shifts' worth of people. The executive VP stepped up on a chair and asked in a higher-pitched voice than usual, "Can everyone hear me?" Then he delivered the news. Bob Borden, Material Tech's president and majority stockholder, had sold his stake in the firm to a private equity group well known for its investments in material sciences. At first, there was stunned silence. There had been no hint of this. No rumors. No water cooler chat. No online blogging speculation. Everybody was taken by surprise.

After the employees had gotten over the initial shock, the inevitable question popped into their minds: *What does this mean to me?* They pondered this as they listened to the executive VP give more details of the transaction. It sounded as if it would be a good thing. Material Tech would continue to operate independently, largely as it had, although the executive VP was becoming president and CEO while Borden assumed the post of nonexecutive chairman. The plant would stay right where it was. There would be no layoffs. There would be fresh capital to make some much-needed equipment purchases to help the company expand. People breathed a little easier.

Then . . . a jaw-dropper. Of the substantial enterprise value Borden personally realized in the capital gain, he had set aside $6 million of his personal proceeds to be distributed among the employees. On average, each one would receive about $20,000 in cash in his or her next paycheck as a partial acknowledgment of that person's role in making the company successful. Once again, there was silence. Then somebody began to clap. More people joined in. Chairs scraped back as a few enthusiasts jumped to their feet. Pretty soon everybody was standing and clapping. There were eyebrows raised, grins and tears of joy and gratitude, whistling, and cheering. The racket went on for a full three minutes.

But Bob Borden was not personally present in the cafeteria to witness the response to his generous action. Later, when I asked him why, he explained that he hadn't done it for the recognition or praise. Besides, he said, public outpourings of emotion always made him uncomfortable. Still, I could tell he was deeply moved. Thirty years earlier, he had started his working life as an hourly employee on Material Tech's manufacturing floor. He had worked his way up through the ranks. As he described it, almost all that was good in his life seemed to somehow have come from his relationship with the company—he had even met his wife, Jacki, there, for goodness sake. There was no question that Borden had earned this wealth creation event, and he and Jacki were committed to recognizing the contribution of all the employees who had helped achieve Material Tech's success. Now he could move on to the next chapter of his life. He told me there were many new challenges he wanted to take on.

Bob Borden is the exception that proves the rule. He had a clear idea of what a positive outcome would look like, for him, his company, his family . . . in fact, for all the stakeholders. But most entrepreneur owner-managers (EOMs) do not have a picture of how they would like things to turn out. They don't begin with the desired end in mind. And frequently as they get closer to it, they're still uncertain what course to take.

Beginning this book with the end is more than a rhetorical tool—it reflects a deeply embedded idea in how I think and interact with clients. Since 1980 my professional home has been Bigelow LLC, where I am a managing director. One hundred percent of my work is with owner-managers who seek to build the value of their enterprises, and to someday capture the wealth they have created in a capital gain transaction. As we work together, what is our desired destination? What is our intended outcome? Starting with the end, let us dream, consider different destinations, set goals, and plan how we might get there. Obviously, no one can predict with precision what will occur in the future; the future is not knowable. And as you'll see, there are aspects to the private capital markets we inhabit that are especially resistant to accurate prediction. The truth is that we, as advisors, can envision what will actually happen at the closing table only a little better than you, the entrepreneur owner-manager, can. What we advisors do know with absolute certainty is that a rich and robust conversation now about your personal life *after* the business transaction—in other words what we term the *simultaneity* of the personal transition and the professional transaction—is directly connected to achieving a successful outcome for the wealth creation transaction.

That means asking and answering questions about your evolving role in your business and how your personal identity is wrapped up in it. It means imagining what life will really be like on the first Monday after the closing. It means picturing the lives of your customers, vendors, and employees; of your partners and your family; of you and your spouse after the new owners are driving the car that you lovingly washed and waxed for so long. And it means learning about how you might manage the newly liquid wealth that will be created in a transaction someday. It means thinking about and exploring a new life purpose, or at the very least, a changed role in the enterprise. Will you imagine it?

Too personal? Too off topic? Hardly. This is personally challenging stuff, but so is building a legacy. I have seen again and again how professional transactions and personal transitions are tightly intertwined. Together they merge as a legacy—*your legacy*. In the pages ahead, I will guide you along the converging pathways of the professional and the personal. I hope to show you how the people I consider to be my best friends and greatest teachers—seasoned, successful owner-managers—are able to earn a fortune *and* simultaneously create a permanent positive legacy. I see this book not so much as a checklist about "how to" but more about the "why to."

If you are a seasoned, successful entrepreneur owner-manager, then acting on what you learn from reading this book will positively change your life. You will learn firsthand details about how other owner-managers like you built and captured a capital gain beyond their wildest expectations, and how they earned a positive legacy that brought them respect of their families and peers that will likely persist for generations. These chapters will share hard-won insights as to how they did it. They will give you direction, which you can then choose to employ (or not). While this book was written for owner-managers, it also applies to expert advisors to owner-managers; you live this every day with your clients.

Plenty of books have been written for would-be entrepreneurs. Some of them are "how-to" books: how to write a business plan, how to raise capital, how to buy a business, how to protect your invention, how to incorporate, and so on. If you are a budding entrepreneur or piloting an early-stage venture, we wish you much luck and good fortune. In this book, you will almost certainly encounter insights that are worth returning to as your journey unfolds, but it wasn't written for you. Nor is this book written for the academic community. To me, the idea of an academician instructing a group of would-be entrepreneurs on the theories of building and capturing enterprise value is rather like a group of novitiates in a monastery talking about sex.

The readers who will find immediate, even life-changing guidance here are seasoned, successful owner-managers—and their professional expert advisors helping them succeed and thrive as the entrepreneurial journey enters its most productive closing chapters. And by the way, when I use the term "owner-manager," I am referring to three related but distinct animals: CEOs with family stockholders, CEO founders, and CEOs with institutional investors. I don't want to cause any misunderstanding that the term *entrepreneur* applies only to start-ups or early-stage ventures.

I focus in these pages on stories of positive successes I have personally witnessed, on owner-managers who strive and ultimately flourish, who give life to our highest hopes, and make the world a better place. Success doesn't necessarily come quickly to them, but, with perseverance and patience, it ultimately does. How did the people who succeeded beyond their wildest dreams do it? Read on.

Most owner-managers are street-smart critical thinkers who value their liberty and independence and don't want a lot of help. Nor, candidly, do they need it. And nothing in this book is to suggest anything about the owner-managers' *operation* of their business or conduct of their personal lives. The genesis of this book is the jolt of energy I feel after a wealth creation transaction when I hear an owner-manager say, "If I'd only known *then* what I know *now*." I've converted that energy to this book in order to give you a glimpse of that care in advance—call it wisdom won out of scar tissue.

What a gift it is for those of us who are owner-managers in the 2010s compared to the 1980s or even the 1990s. Technology has leveled the playing field between large and small firms, and the advantage enjoyed since the 1950s by large hierarchical bureaucratic organizations has diminished. But it is more important than ever to have a clear idea of your desired outcome, because the private transaction market (where we play, and about which I will go into detail later in the book) has become highly complex, with asymmetrical information and sophisticated investors who typically have much more experience in the market than owner-managers. In the 1980s, the standard transaction involved an owner-manager who had reached the end of his career and wanted to sell the business. The typical purchaser was a strategic investor, usually operating within the same industry, who would buy the entire company and assimilate that organization's operations into its own. The owner-manager got a payout and made his exit. It wasn't until the end of the 1980s that private equity groups (PEGs) were invented and came on the scene. They provided a new source of capital as well as a new style of investment. They are not interested in a 100 percent purchase of a company or in managing operations. They act more like a partner—a highly focused and motivated partner—than a traditional buyer.

The merger and acquisition (M&A) advisor role has changed, too. It used to be that you could choose to work with a smaller advisory firm, which had the benefit of being local and, thanks to its size, might give you individualized attention. Or you could go with one of the large, legacy, logo Wall Street firms. They sold themselves on their expertise with bigger transactions, access to proprietary financial data, and dedicated research staffs.

I am not objective about all of this, as you can imagine, but it's clear to nearly everyone that the big M&A advisory firms no longer have an inherent advantage. Scrappy boutique M&A advisory firms have access to the same databases and get the same information on every company in the world at exactly the same time as the Wall Street firms do. What's more, the economy of scale that may once have been an advantage for the big firms is now, I believe, a diseconomy of scale. These firms are so big and bureaucratic they are unskilled at advising private owner-managed companies that are a fraction of their size and are run by hands-on leaders with skin in the game rather than corporate caretaker/employees. They simply do not understand or empathize with the challenges of owner-managed private enterprises, they are not organized for them, nor for the most part are they effective with them.

Not only do the investors and advisors look different today, the profile of typical owner-managers has also changed and will continue to do so. These owner-managers are planning and achieving their business transitions earlier in their lives. Some build more than one business and go through more than one wealth creation event. They're living longer and have greater expectations for the years that used to be called retirement.

We're seeing a rapid gender shift in owner-managers. More and more women will be making legacy decisions for the companies they have created and built. Although most of the seasoned successful entrepreneur owner-managers I have met in my practice so far have been men, I am happy to say that my intuition, and some good data, tells me those days are over. A recent study by the Kauffmann Foundation[1] found that 30 percent of the owners of entrepreneurial firms are women. It reported that men and women see the challenges facing entrepreneurs the same way, that women have no more difficulty raising the financial resources necessary than men do, and that women have always wanted to be part of an entrepreneurial culture. In fact, in the study, women were more likely than men to say that "working for someone else doesn't appeal to me." Add to the equation the growing education advantage that women have and it is clear to me that women will soon close the entrepreneurial "gap."

We are living and working in an era of great change and huge potential. Over the next two decades, we're going to see a monumental shift in ownership along with the largest transfer of wealth in history. There is so much opportunity ahead that more buyers—and new types of buyers—are flooding onto the scene from all over the world with vast amounts of capital to invest specifically in successful privately owned businesses.

In writing this book, I realize that the number of companies my firm and I have worked with directly—our sample size—is relatively small, and the work is necessarily qualitative; our knowledge can never be complete. So I have attempted to weave in insights from the most gifted and influential thought leaders who play at the intersection of entrepreneurship, psychology, finance, and probability theory, including Marty Seligman, Danny Kahneman, E. O. Wilson, David Brooks, Steven Rollnick, Nassim Taleb, Peter

Drucker, Barry Schwartz, Michael Mauboussin, Angela Duckworth, Clay Christensen, Atul Gawande, Richard Zeckhauser, and Chris Peterson.

Still, although my sample size may be small, given the total number of transactions that have taken place in the past 30 years, I have met thousands of successful owner-managers and have had the opportunity to consult closely with hundreds of them. I have energetically pursued my career—actually, I think of it as a calling—because I believe that the entrepreneur owner-manager of a private enterprise is one of the most important pro-economic, and pro-social forces on the planet. That is because everybody shares in the massive capital gains created through the recapitalization or sale of these companies. The liquidity they generate quite literally funds the entire philanthropic not-for-profit sector as well as investment in new enterprises. Think that is a bold claim? A quick glance at the names of the hundred largest private charitable foundations provides ample proof that it is true: Gates, Buffett, Ford, Getty, Johnson, Hewlett, Kellogg, Lilly, Packard, MacArthur, Moore. Every single one began as an entrepreneur owner-manager.

Those entrepreneurial fortunes—indeed, all sustainable wealth—is created in just one way: by the efforts of owner-managers captured in a capital gain. Entrepreneurial fortunes do not arise from the net profit of their enterprise being "saved up" and invested in a bank account or even in some other investment or business. Instead, fortunes are almost always created as a result of a capital gain, that is, the discounted value of the future stream of excess cash returns in your concentrated, risky, illiquid, private business. Realizing the fortune you have built in your company is not as simple as riding your industry and watching the business grow. It requires identifying the drivers of enterprise value in your industry and ferociously concentrating all your resources on them. The brilliance of entrepreneurial capitalism is that the system allows selfish goals at the individual level to be converted into highly positive and constructive results for the greater good of the community as a whole.

Why should all this matter to us? Well, according to government statistics, fully half of all businesses fail before their fifth year. I know from hard personal experience that when a company goes under, it generates negative energy: sorrow and woe, lost jobs, lost investment, demands for personal guarantees, scuffles with banks and investors, abandoned real estate, shattered dreams, and broken hearts. Even when a business does go the distance, the reward may not be as great as it could be. Far too many private business owners don't focus on or don't know how to optimize the enterprise value of their businesses, nor do they understand how to capture it, even if they have created it. We need private enterprise to "secure the economy's future" and, I would add, we need private businesses to create as much wealth as they possibly can for all stakeholders.

That is why I wrote this book. As I've said, I can't count the number of times owner-managers have said to me, "Pete, if only I had known then, when I was running the company, what I know now, after I've sold it, I would have done so many things differently."

These owner-managers are some of the most positive, generous, caring, demanding, energy creating, challenging, and tirelessly persistent people in the world. They are my best friends. I like them as people, and I empathize with just how hard it is to go to work day after day with their capital at risk, managing through the people issues, technical issues, and regulatory issues to build an enterprise of hundreds of employees and tens of millions of enterprise value designed to last forever. I hope my empathy, appreciation, and affection are evident throughout these pages.

Why does the architecture of this book start with the end? This method creates a potential destination; it informs readers through real-life narratives drawn from my 30-plus years of working with owner-managers and their expert advisors. It is supported by the practical applications of the leading edge of theoretical foundations from psychology and finance. Can a rigorous methodology be created and applied that prepares owner-managers to capture—both psychologically and financially—their hard-earned wealth in a capital gain and create a positive legacy? Yes it can. Although such a methodology will not be found in the conventional corporate finance literature, I offer it in this book. It is based upon my years of helping our clients to identify and build on their corporate and individual strengths so they position their enterprises and themselves to achieve optimal organizational success and live their lives to the fullest.

A Brief Guide to the Book

In Chapter 1, "The Unique Character of the Entrepreneur Owner-Manager," and Chapter 2, "Four Hats, One Head, Big Challenge," I examine the character, roles, and thinking styles of the entrepreneur owner-manager. It sounds theoretical, and there is a bit of theory involved, but it is mostly practical. I start the book this way because I have found that owner-managers, not having been exposed to character assessment tools, are not always aware of the fundamental nature of the entrepreneur and of the decision-making biases the entrepreneur is often prone to. This understanding may not be of great importance while you are building a business, but it becomes critical when planning and executing a wealth creation event and company transition. If you don't understand how your own approach and method of making decisions differ from those of your advisors and potential new majority owners, it's easy to make mistakes and operate under incorrect assumptions.

In Chapter 3, "Creating Enterprise Value," we get down to brass tacks, as I address the fundamental question: how do you assure the longevity of your enterprise beyond your personal ownership of it? In this chapter, I examine the practice of enterprise value building by considering the four questions that you will be asked—and must be able to positively answer—when the discussions with potential investors begin: (1) Is your industry in or out of favor with institutional investors? (2) Do you have a simple, clear, and coherent business plan? (3) Does your superior financial performance validate your strategy? (4) Can we find the best-fit investor who has a compelling reason to invest now? This is the heart of the matter. Start here, if you want.

In Chapter 4, "Seller Beware: The Private Transaction Market," I provide an overview of the private transaction market and the key players who you will interact with there: the strategic investors, private equity groups, and private equity platforms. It is very important to understand the market you are entering, because you will be dealing with high-powered, highly professional, coldly objective investors with lots of experience in company assessment and deal making. You need to be armed with as much information and knowledge as you can take in before you begin to work with your advisor to identify a best-fit investor.

In Chapter 5, "Capturing Enterprise Value," I take you through the entire transaction, starting with what you need to do and know before you even start to talk with potential investors, how and why to engage your management team, what you're looking for in an investor, and the stages of the transaction.

In Chapter 6, "Creating a Positive Legacy," I delve into a topic that is rarely discussed and almost completely ignored by entrepreneur owner-managers who are contemplating a company transition: what comes after the event takes place? I have observed that owner-managers are wildly underprepared for the next chapter of their lives and go through four predictable postsale stages: realization, hibernation, experimentation, and reinvention. Although it's impossible to fully prepare yourself for what's to come, a better understanding of the issues can make the transition much easier and more fruitful for all involved.

In the concluding chapter, "The Beginning of the Legacy," I list six things you can do *right now* to start building the value of your enterprise and preparing for a company transition, and a bit of philosophy on why your efforts are so valuable and important—not just to you, but to all of those around you and to our society as a whole.

As I stated in my author's note, stories I tell in this book are all true. There are no "composite" stories or made-up tall tales to "make a point." All involve real people in real-life situations, real companies, and real capital gain transactions, although the names and identifying details have been disguised to guard the privacy of my friends and clients.

A final word before you dive in. You are approaching the largest and most important challenge of your career. It's usually the largest single financial event in your life. Who you choose to become the next majority investor in your business will have a great deal of impact on your legacy and on the lives of all stakeholders. It's a decision you have never faced before, and you may never have another chance to get it right. This is no time for teaching error. You want to successfully overcome the challenges you will encounter on this journey so you can be delivered to a positive and generative legacy, to a place where you are rich and enriched—an ending made clear in the beginning.

There is no doubt that after reading and absorbing this book you will know more about building and capturing enterprise value, and creating positive legacy than the vast majority of all the people in the world. There's a stake in the ground for you. Let's get started.

1

The Unique Character of the Entrepreneur Owner-Manager

The Secret of Victory lies not wholly with superior knowledge.
It lurks invisible in that Vital Spark,
intangible, yet as evident as lightning.
—GEORGE S. PATTON, JR.

MEET TED CHANDLER, PEACE CORPS VOLUNTEER, A DOCTOR OF anthropology, founder of an international development advisory firm called UCT, and a dyed-in-the-wool entrepreneur owner-manager (EOM). What does that mean? What are the character traits of this unique species of human being? What are the strengths of these individuals? How do they think?

Why does it matter? It matters because it's important for you, as an owner-manager, to know your strengths and your biases as you build your organization and think about a capital gain event someday. And it's equally important, probably more important, for EOM's expert advisors and investors to understand what makes the owner-manager tick so they can get to the best outcome together, with the least bafflement possible.

Ted Chandler followed a very different path than Bob Borden (whom we met in the Introduction) did, but the two men have a lot in common. Ted was born in the Midwest and as a young man did a stint as a volunteer in the Peace Corps in Ghana. There, with his heart opened and his mind illuminated, he realized that being able to make a difference for the better in people's lives was his True North. He seriously considered signing on with the Peace Corps as a full-time professional employee but, on closer inspection, saw a culture that rewarded the politically shrewd over the personally passionate.

Still searching, Ted went back to school, earned a PhD in anthropology, and then decided entrepreneurship was the way for him to make a big positive difference in people's lives. He founded a small consulting firm that advised developing nations in the domains of agriculture, environment, water, democracy, antiterrorism, and other areas related to infrastructure—the same areas that fascinated him as a Peace Corps volunteer. He did not abandon his True North; if anything, he dedicated more energy and capital to it. And the company was successful, effective on the ground, attracting world-class talent, and growing. UCT eventually employed hundreds of people and established dozens of offices around the world, successfully carrying out large complex projects that changed people's lives for the better in Africa and around the globe.

So far, so good. But UCT's growth had also generated a familiar conundrum: As people grew and took on new responsibilities within the organization, they also moved away from their unique competencies. People who had been effective in the field proved to be less so as managers; a brilliant water management engineer isn't necessarily the right person to manage a team of 20 environmental engineers.

There wasn't a shortage of professional managers who could do the basics—keeping an office organized and on task—but UCT's mission was loftier than that. Too many professional managers were unable to hear the authentic heartbeat of the company.

By the time I first met Ted, there was no doubt this chapter of his personal journey was ending. By "ending" I don't mean winding down while he consulted and advised new owners; I mean *Ted wanted out.* He wanted to hand over the ownership responsibility to a great new majority owner—one who would be a terrific fit and fully in tune with the mission—and be personally liberated to walk out the door and into the next chapter of his life. He knew exactly how he wanted that story to go. He wanted to spend more time with his wife, kids, and grandkids at their place in Costa Rica, and to execute on some important global philanthropic interests he shared with his wife. He was seriously considering getting back to his love: being in the field through another volunteer stint with the Peace Corps. Ted, more than any other owner-manager I have met, came to our initial discussion clear that he was driven to achieve his personal transition and professional transaction simultaneously, and in a specific type of way.

When I gently suggested that I admired his vision but that the next owners would appreciate—and pay for—his counsel during the transition, Ted focused his piercing gray eyes into mine and calmly, quietly, and forcefully said, "You are not hearing me, Worrell. No matter who the investor is, I am *out* day one. If I had wanted a 'partner,' I would have had one by now. If you're saying you can't pull that off, or that it's improbable, tell me now. If that's how it is, I may just have to wind down the operation and liquidate the assets instead." Ted was nothing if not definite and straightforward.

In this case, liquidating the assets was a viable alternative, given the service nature of the business—there was no plant or equipment, no inventory, and few fixed costs. But there were the employees to think about, as well as the vital work they were performing for the customers the company had gained over the years with its name and reputation. Those two factors kept Ted from going down the road of liquidation.

We set to work. Part of my role was to help Ted configure the organization so he could make a clean departure. We immediately promoted one of his senior managers to president/CEO, moved Ted into the chairman role, and brought his five most senior managers immediately into the discussion of what lay ahead. They were the ones who would have to execute the business plan with the new owner, so they had to be ready—in fact, it had to be their plan.

We prepared materials on UCT that were very candid about Ted's posttransaction desires: he would exit, or there would be no deal. We crafted an engagement architecture that resulted in Ted having choices between the types of investors who wanted to become the next majority owner of UCT—a private equity platform company and a publicly owned West Coast–based strategic investor. Ted encouraged his management team to voice their opinions on the best fit, while he kept his favorite to himself. In the end, they all agreed on becoming a wholly owned part of a strategic investor. Now, a few years later, under its ownership and with the leadership of the management team Ted had put in place, UCT has more than doubled in size. Ted earned a fortune and now allocates his personal energy as he had envisioned he would.

A Rare Breed

Owner-managers of private enterprises, such as Ted Chandler and Bob Borden, are a rare breed. Every owner-manager is a unique animal, and, without a doubt, every transaction he or she engages in is different. But in the three decades I've been serving and learning from the leaders of private companies, my colleagues and I have observed some consistent character strengths. Owner-managers are some of the most positive, generous, caring, demanding, energy-creating, and persistent people in the world. They go to work day after day and deal with all the hands-on tasks and responsibilities of management: people issues, technical concerns, regulatory complications, and so on. Their energies and reputations are on the line, and their personal capital is at risk—that is, they have "skin in the game." Many of them build enterprises that employ hundreds of people and create tens of millions of dollars of value.

At the same time, the set of strengths, characteristics, biases, and decision-making approaches that enable the owner-manager to overcome challenges and build valuable enterprises may not be so helpful when it comes to capturing value and transitioning the company. Among those traits, entrepreneur owner-managers tend not to be highly introspective or self-examining, so they may have a harder time dealing with the emotional, psychological, and behavioral issues involved with such fundamental life changes. Just like Bob Borden, they don't deal so well with being thrown into the limelight or enduring gushy scenes. In this regard, Ted Chandler was the exception that proved the rule: he had a high level of self-awareness.

The Top Five Character Strengths

For many years, as I gained experience in this field and became more and more intimately involved with seasoned, successful entrepreneurs, I grew curious about their character. (See Figure 1.1.) Are they really different from other people in the general population, or do they just seem that way? If they are different, what components of

FIGURE 1.1   Character Strengths of Entrepreneur Owner-Managers

character are specific to entrepreneurs? Are there common strengths they possess or develop? Is there causation? And, just as important, what is it that people get *wrong* about entrepreneurs? What flawed assumptions are overdue for a challenge?

I looked for answers in the emerging field of positive psychology, a field that has developed new insights into optimal performance. Unlike traditional psychology, positive psychology does not concern itself with disorders or dysfunctions but rather focuses on the study of positive human qualities, the strengths or characteristics that give people advantage in their functioning and performance. This stuff matters. Studies have shown that positive emotions actually change how your mind works—and the effects are nonlinear. Effects that are nonexistent at a starting point grow disproportionately large. Sharpening the focus on positive characteristics and emotions broadens and builds your resources for future thriving. Flourishing people perform at exceptionally high levels and add value to organizations.

In 2009, I led my colleagues at Bigelow to kick off original research to try to answer our questions about entrepreneurial character. We sought guidance from three scholars well-known for their work in the field of positive psychology: Martin E. P. Seligman, Chris Peterson, and Angela Duckworth, all of whom are associated with the University of Pennsylvania. Seligman is the acknowledged founder of the positive psychology approach and, with Mihaly "Mike" Csikszentmihalyi (author of *Flow*), wrote a definitive introduction on the subject of Positive Psychology, in the periodical *American Psychologist.*[1]

Based partly on their insights and advice, we conducted our research with the help of a standardized positive psychology assessment tool called the Values in Action Inventory of Strengths (VIA-IS). More than 1.3 million people have taken the survey since 2001 (viacharacter.org/surveys.aspx) which is a very large sample. We used a questionnaire called "The VIA Brief Inventory of Strengths," created by Chris Peterson and Martin Seligman, that asks the respondents to rate themselves on each of 24 traits on a scale of 1 to 5.

In addition, we wanted to take a closer look at a characteristic we believe is key to entrepreneurs but is not included on the VIA-IS classification: Dr. Duckworth and her colleagues define *grit* as "passion and perseverance for long-term goals." To measure that trait, we used a second survey called "The Short Grit Scale" (Grit-S). Respondents were asked to answer four questions pertaining to their consistency of interests, and four questions pertaining to their persistence of effort.

For our research, we recruited some 200 seasoned, successful entrepreneurs and advisors to them. The advisors who participated were asked to complete the survey as if they were answering for their entrepreneur clients. We did not pay or compensate the respondents.

The results illustrated in Figure 1.1 are illuminating about the character of owner-managers, largely because they were so consistent across the group and because they aligned with my experience with and understanding of these people. Of the 24 character strengths, these are the 5 most common among the owner-managers in our sample:

1. *Authenticity.* Most seasoned successful owner-managers embody this trait of being genuine and real. They speak the truth as they see it. They act without pretense, and they take responsibility for their feelings and actions. They own their own stories (even the messy ones). They don't usually cover up their vulnerability or their humanness. When Ted Chandler looked me in the eye and said, "I want out," I had no doubt he meant it; he was willing to risk being very transparent with me.

2. *Leadership.* Leadership is about encouraging a group of which you're a member to get things done by maintaining good relations within the group. I watched as Chandler did this by using his attracting personality to recruit, build, and retain his senior management team.

3. *Fairness.* Fairness is treating all people the same way according to notions of fairness and justice, not letting your personal feelings bias decisions about others, and giving everyone a fair shot at success. I think Bob Borden exemplified this trait, partly because he had experienced it for himself, as he climbed the ladder from shop-floor worker to president of the company.

4. *Gratitude.* Gratitude is being aware of and thankful for the good things that happen and, importantly, taking time to express your thanks. Throughout his career, Bob Borden was known for this characteristic. He expressed it in many little ways over the years, and in dramatic fashion at the end: with an unexpected and generous cash payment to recognize the contributions of all employees.

5. *Zest.* Zest is a combination of vitality, enthusiasm, vigor, energy, and excitement. This rings very true for owner-managers. They don't do things halfway or halfheartedly. Life is an adventure for them.[2]

Over time, my hypothesis is that people who exhibit these kinds of positive character strengths don't simply reflect success; focusing on these characteristics can also produce success.

Plus Grit!

Now on to that additional and intriguing trait: grit.

According to the work of Angela Duckworth and her colleagues, grit is a combination of passion and persistence for long-term goals. It is not, as the word might suggest, merely grind-it-out stick-to-itiveness regardless of task. Grit comes from within, and those people who have it aren't particularly dependent on feedback or praise from others. Grit endures—and even strengthens—in the face of challenges and in response to setbacks.

I view grit as an alchemical combination of enthusiasm, persistence, and motivation. Perhaps the persistence is related to their willingness to fail, make a course correction, and continue on their journey. Certainly, the most successful entrepreneurs are the ones who persist and adjust long after others might rationally call it a day. To paraphrase William James, seasoned entrepreneurs seem to have found their second wind—they have tapped a new level of energy. Sure, other types of people manage to get a "second wind" in their careers, but not everybody does, and it doesn't happen very often. Many of the most successful owner-managers live in the second wind, and they have a third, fourth, and fifth wind too.

Decision-Making Biases

Now I'd like to turn to something a little different: some other characteristics that I have persistently observed in my work with entrepreneur owner-managers. You can think of these simply as shortcut habits of mind or, in more technical language, they are called decision-making biases.

At the beginning of my career, when I witnessed friends and clients making decisions that were obviously not in their own best interest, I thought they were probably anomalies. After a number of years, however, I realized they weren't anomalies; in fact, they were systematic, repetitive, and somewhat predictable. I did not have the technical vocabulary then to accurately describe what I saw until I discovered the work of Daniel Kahneman and Amos Tversky in the 1980s. I was thrilled that I found experts who were able to articulately describe and scientifically test the notions I had only fleetingly glimpsed in my mind's eye, and which I had struggled to completely describe to others. With their work, behavioral finance was born, and Kahneman and Tversky became two of my heroes. A psychologist awarded the Nobel Prize in Economics? (This is interesting stuff. Kahneman won the Nobel Prize in 2002 for work he did with Tversky; Tversky could not be awarded the prize, as the Nobel Committee doesn't award posthumously.) And it is clearly relevant to the neighborhood we live in—at the intersection of psychology and finance.

Like many others, I studied classical economics as an undergraduate, and I was taught that for the purposes of thinking about economic decision making in domains of risk, humans act as "Homo Economicus"—the strictly rational decision maker. In fact, people are typically more driven by emotions than they are by rationality and economics. To make this point, the behavioral economist Dick

Thaler humorously divides the world into two types of people: the "Humans" and the "Econs." Owner-managers are of the Human species; their decision making is inherently emotional. Investors, on the other hand (who are usually agents), tend to be more coolly rational Econs.

When you're thinking about a capital gain transaction, it's essential for you—the owner-manager, the potential investor or acquirer, and the advisors for both sides—to understand this different orientation toward decision making in risky environments. Econs tend to think Humans are mostly influenced by money, and Humans tend to assume the Econs understand the emotions involved. Neither assumption is accurate.

Why do these authentic, bright, savvy, ambitious creatures make these seemingly obvious decision-making errors that potentially affect their legacy and wealth in negative ways? The decision-making process is rarely rational, as psychologists define the word, almost always involves intense emotions, and is usually subject to one or more of the decision-making biases (as that term is used in behavioral finance). I began to realize my colleagues and I could almost systematically predict the decision-making mistakes these owner-managers would make based upon my observations of them and their environment. Behavioral finance gives us a dozen or so basic decision-making errors. Let me briefly describe six of the key ones here that my experience tells me are most applicable to EOMs, because I will be referring to them throughout the book.

Negativity Bias

A key aspect of the psychology of the owner-manager—indeed, it is a characteristic we all share—that affects her when playing the four roles of the owner-manager (CEO, owner, family member, individual—which we'll examine in the next chapter) is *negativity bias.* This simply means that, in most situations, "bad" feels much worse than the same quantity of "good" feels good. Negativity bias comes into play when the owner-manager's roles come into conflict, causing her to make decisions and strategic choices that may make life easier in the short term but limit enterprise value in the long run.

From an evolutionary point of view, this makes sense. If primitive humans ran away from bad things or events (for example, predators), they got to live another day. People use up disproportionately large amounts of energy trying to escape bad emotions or bad moods. In fact, there is a wealth of research that concludes that "bad" feels about 2.5 times stronger than "good." Or said another way, a 10 percent loss creates as powerful a negative feeling as a 25 percent gain creates a positive one. The tendency obviously, is to ruminate over bad events, to feel small losses more acutely than equally sized gains. Both habits can cause unreasonable amounts of anxiety and propel you to make decisions that are not in the best interest of your stakeholders or of building your enterprise value.

Loss Aversion

Loss aversion has to do with variations from expected behaviors when people are making decisions involving risk. Risky decisions are those that have a probability of a gain or a loss in your business. The probable gain or loss need not be financial; it can involve image, reputation, prestige, celebrity, other kinds of assets, opportunities, or whatever. For our purposes, however, let's use money.[3]

The identification of loss aversion is one of the outcomes of a breakthrough developed by Kahneman and Tversky in 1979, who called it "prospect theory." They showed that people—in this case, business owners—don't rationally consider decisions based upon the probable resultant state of their enterprise value or net worth. Rather they measure from a reference point of what they believe their enterprise value or net worth to be right now. In other words, business owners think in terms of gains and losses from a reference point, not in terms of an absolute state of wealth. What's even more significant is that owners will take more risk in order to avoid a loss, from their reference point, than they will to achieve a gain. Hear me on this: *most people will take on more risk to avoid a loss than they will for the expectation of the same magnitude of gain.*

For owner-managers, loss aversion intensifies over time—as there is more and more at stake and thus more to lose. I have had many discussions with owner-managers who began their career arc with no capital, no image, no name, and no assets. At that time, they were willing to risk everything. Later in the arc of their lives, they have built an enterprise value that is so high it surprises them. And they become loss averse. They become less willing to take on risk to achieve an incremental increase in the enterprise value because they are afraid of losing some of it now that they "know" what it is worth. (Of course, they don't *really* know until the transaction is complete.) When Ted Chandler got to a certain stage in his life, he no longer was willing to "bet the farm" for future increases in enterprise value. In fact, he was willing to liquidate the enterprise value in order not to risk it any further. He really wanted to move to the next chapter of his life.

Anchoring Bias

When owner-managers are asked to make a risky decision, they typically use some starting point as a "given." They then consider the decision in relation to that starting point. The starting point might be clearly stated, such as an asking price for a piece of real estate. Or, it might merely be suggested by the way the decision is presented. Both are artificial, but they take root in the mind. Behavioral finance scholars have consistently found that relatively different starting points result in absolutely different decisions. Thus, using a "given" as a starting point for making any decision always results in a less-than-objective decision.

This is anchoring bias. The starting point is the anchor, and it can be very difficult to unchain yourself from it. Any time a number is suggested as a possible result of a decision you are trying to make (for example, asking price, possible salary, or cost of service), anchoring bias kicks in. Once an anchor is set, almost everyone adjusts less than they should when they are thinking about the decision outcome. Kahneman believes anchoring bias affects professionals and nonprofessionals equally.

One of my favorite examples is a scientific study of real estate agents who were given the chance to estimate the value of a property going on the market. Some of the agents were shown the property with a high asking price; others saw the same property listing, but with a low asking price. When the agents were asked to give their coldly unbiased objective view of the fair market value of the property (after studying an objective comprehensive market study that included other comparables), the correlation was astoundingly high between those who saw a high asking price and those who estimated high fair market value. That's something our grandmother could have taught us, right? You should know that if there is an offer on the table, you will be subject to an anchoring bias, just because the number is there.

Availability Bias

Most of us are terrible at dealing with probability, even though we encounter countless decisions every day whose optimal outcome depends on accurate probabilistic thinking. We are deluged with data, and it is difficult to separate signal from noise. So it is no surprise that when facing a risky decision we frequently rely on information that most readily comes to mind. But just because the information is conveniently available in our memories does not mean it is most applicable to the specific case. Often the information that is most available is that which has been provided to us most vividly, most repeatedly, and most frequently by people who are lively and who tell us about memorable events. We instinctively use information that is most available in our memories instead of using information that is most applicable to the problem at hand.

Consider the following scene. A successful founder-entrepreneur is talking to some friends at a conference of successful business owners. He goes on about the possibility of achieving a capital gain someday. He says that he is thinking about retaining a nationally known executive search firm to seek a world-class CFO for his business.

Some of his listeners tell him he is making a big mistake. "I just saw an article in the *Wall Street Journal*," says one. "Everybody knows that the CFO is the first to go after an acquisition by a strategic acquirer."

"Right," says another, "And you'll want a strategic acquirer because it always pays the highest price."

There are two things going on here, neither good. First, it is not true that strategic acquirers always offer the highest values. (More on that later.) Second, our business owner and his friends are succumbing to availability bias in their thinking about the CFO hire. They are responding to information that is readily recalled or is easily at hand. Yes, there may have been a piece in the *Journal* about a CFO being replaced, but that does not mean that all CFOs are the first to go after an acquisition. This is a narrative fallacy. All too often, the availability bias causes us to think that the probability of something memorable happening again is greater than it actually is.

Availability bias makes us ignore probability and causes us to make bad decisions.

Endowment Effect

As an owner-manager, are you willing to buy your business today at the same value you would agree to sell it for today? If not, you probably are under the influence of the endowment effect.

This bias, originally hypothesized by Dick Thaler in 1980 and related to Samuelson and Zeckhauser's status quo bias (1988), has special significance for you as an owner-manager. According to traditional economic theory, the rational person (the Econ) should be willing to buy an asset for the same amount for which she or he would sell it. Behavioral finance studies, however, consistently show that the minimum selling price that owners state for an asset almost always exceeds the maximum purchase price they are willing to pay for the same assets. Effectively then (scratching our heads), ownership of an asset in and of itself "endows" the asset with some ethereal added value from the owner's point of view.

More complexity is introduced to endowment bias when a business is inherited. Often in these situations, owner-managers say they have feelings of distress, disloyalty, or even shame associated with considering new ownership alternatives for a business bequeathed from a previous generation. They are confused by what is "the right thing to do," and at what value. Endowment bias influences owner-managers to hold onto businesses they have inherited, often regardless of whether that decision is in the best interest of the owner-manager or of the business itself. Occasionally, endowment bias results in decision paralysis. For example, one owner-manager, having placed an irrational premium on a business that he inherited, slowly liquidates the business year by year, not by doing anything explicit, but just through his inaction.[4]

People do not feel a sense of endowment about all their assets. Consider a $1,000 certificate of deposit (CD). If you are offered $1,000 cash for the $1,000 CD, you do not feel any endowment bias because you hold that CD with the expectation of trading it one day. Similarly, research has shown that experienced traders are less susceptible to endowment bias because they view an asset merely as a store of wealth they hold for the very purpose of trading. Further, empirical evidence proves that trading experience in markets matters greatly when trying to solve for this bias. Across all asset types, market-specific experience and the magnitude of endowment effect are inversely correlated.

These insights are meaningful for you as an owner-manager who is contemplating life in the private transaction market. If you have significant merger and acquisition experience, endowment effect decreases even to the point of being negligible. But few owner-managers have this depth of experience, and often they are not aware of their endowment bias. As a result, they will enter the private transaction market and negotiate on their own behalf with professional investors. Investors are generally Econs, coldly objective about their intent to trade their investment in the future, and often they are acting as agents for a larger entity, such as a private equity group. Owner-managers without a great deal of experience find themselves at a significant disadvantage in these situations because they are influenced by the endowment effect.

Overconfidence Bias

Almost all of us overestimate what we think we know, and we often are confident even when we're wrong. This overconfidence bias has a confusing and wicked effect. Highly successful owner-managers sometimes equate success with being right—and believe there is a correlation: *I am confident I am right, and as proof just look at my successful result.* Luck or good timing had nothing to do with it.

Experts are particularly dangerous in this regard because they are often trained to be confident even when they are uncertain. Sometimes groups of people who have gone to the same elite schools and have been taught the same dogma—for example, efficient market theory, mean-variance optimization, efficient frontier, just in time, and total quality management—drink the overconfidence Kool-Aid. The ultrarational Econ point of view is the proud theme of our professional schools. By using better "processes" we will arrive at better decision-making results, right? Yeah, right.

There is plenty of research that shows how informed, intelligent people will regularly and repeatedly overestimate their abilities— both to predict outcomes and to make judgments based on information they have been given. Very few of us consistently use probabilistic thinking, by which we attempt to rationally estimate the probabilities of certain outcomes, and then multiply them against the results of those outcomes, resulting in an expected value for a given decision. Instead, we often think we are smarter and have more precise information than we actually do. And since owner-managers are naturally optimistic, we sometimes underestimate possible downside risks. Because we are overconfident, we may not be well prepared for a future post–wealth creation transaction, and underestimate the very real personal challenges that are outlined in detail in Chapter 6.

Two Things Entrepreneurs Are Not: Big Risk Takers or Corporate Chieftains

I mentioned misconceptions that people have about entrepreneurs. One of them is that these people are big risk takers, and the second is that they have a lot in common with the CEOs of big public firms. Untrue on both counts.

Let's start with risk. Bigelow and a team from Harvard's Kennedy School have completed groundbreaking research showing that seasoned, successful entrepreneurs are not risk takers at all. In fact, they are highly risk averse. This research (the only of its kind that we know of) measures the risk tolerance of owner-managers and their expert advisors in real-life risky business decisions (with nominal monetary payoffs). It shows that to take a risky choice, entrepreneurs typically require a probability of success that is roughly two times higher than break-even. The obvious conclusion is that entrepreneur owner-managers are risk *avoiders*, an image totally contrary to the general public's or the media's depiction of them. They do take what others would consider to be a big risk simply by deciding to follow the unconventional path of owning their own company in a very specific domain. But once they do that, they focus on reducing risk as much as possible. The media tends to interpret that unconventional choice as a risk. But entrepreneurs see themselves as ill-suited for conventional jobs, and they are more willing to avoid or quit seemingly safe paths in the bureaucratic economy to launch and lead ventures that seem risky to those with more conventional professional aspirations. What seems safe to others might be risky to the person with the entrepreneurial bent. And what seems risky to others seems safer for them. To entrepreneurs the *real* risk frequently resides in what others view as safe, or conventional, choices.

By contrast, the corporate executive views risk very differently. The entrepreneur owner-manager and the corporate CEO of a public company are completely different animals. The owner-manager thinks of what she does as a calling and regards her company as family. The corporate CEO views what he does as a profession and considers himself to be an agent for the stockholders. Some corporate

CEOs have negotiated big financial gains without the company performance one would expect. Owner-managers, on the other hand, have their capital (usually nearly all of it) at risk. There are no golden parachutes and no stock option plans. If the business fails, they lose everything. If the business succeeds, they succeed. When success or failure of the business is tied directly to your personal economic success, it tends to focus the mind.

Midwest Tool: What Should Have Looked Good, Felt Bad

Let me end this chapter with a story that went quite differently from that of Bob Borden, the president of Material Tech who distributed $6 million to his employees, and of Ted Chandler, who successfully achieved the freedom of the next chapter. This one is a sad story.

Jim Ross was the second-generation owner-manager of Midwest Tool, a manufacturer of composite hand tools. His father, Dick, had emigrated to the United States in the early 1950s from England with the legendary 25 cents in his pocket. Dick noticed that construction hand tools were in high demand, and he thought that composite hand tools would be a lot more handy and inexpensive than metal ones. Dick was a character. He had all the character strengths of seasoned successful entrepreneurs in spades—authenticity, fairness, leadership, gratitude, and, most of all, zest—a really attracting person with an infectious love of life. He knew a little something about molding composites, and he assembled the capital and the team. Forty years later, he had a company with over $200 million in revenues generated from four manufacturing plants across North America.

After six years of college, Dick's son Jim started in the business as a salesman, and he wasn't terrible at it. But he could never muster the passion for the business that clearly came naturally to his dad. He didn't seem to be blessed with the same character strengths as his dad, nor was grit much in evidence in his toolkit. Over time, father Dick gifted the stock of the business equally to son Jim and Jim's sister Nora. Then, when Dick was 82, Midwest Tool was approached by a private equity group that had a platform company in the composites industry. The platform company envisioned a scenario in which it would tuck Midwest Tool into its structure and go-forward plan. Through the usual series of meetings, a verbal offer was made of nearly $100 million, and the other terms were agreed to with a handshake. No merger and acquisition advisor was involved.

One morning, about three weeks after the handshake, Dick walked into Jim's office. He said, "Jim, I have good news–bad news. The good news is I talked to our sales VP, Lee, last night. Boy, he's terrific, isn't he? That guy can sell. He was in Bentonville, and we have a big new order coming in from you-know-who." *Great*, Jim thought grimly to himself, fully aware of the miniscule gross margin Midwest Tool made on orders from that company.

Dick continued. "Now for the bad news. I am afraid you are going to be really disappointed, but I just cannot go through with the plan to sell the business. I haven't slept a wink in the past week. I won't be able to live with myself if I sell the business to this private equity group [more about them in Chapter 4] that is going to shut some plants, reengineer our overhead, and fire people here at headquarters. I hired all these people, Jimmy. They are like family to me—no, they *are* my family. Besides, where am I going to go every day if I have to retire and don't have this place to come to? This is where I have all my fun. I love being with these people and spending time thinking about the new plant layout and what the new product development rollout is going to be at the next trade show! I thought of two great new products just last night!"

Case closed. No sale. Negotiations ended.

A year or so later, after suffering a stroke on the tennis court, Dick passed away. Naturally, son Jim became the CEO of the company. But the industry was rapidly changing. Oil prices rose and, as a consequence, costs of plastic resin composite prices rose steadily too. During Dick's time, the company used to have dozens of suppliers of resin, but the number of suppliers had dwindled to four. The long-term relationships Dick fostered no longer seemed to make any difference; in fact, all the suppliers seemed to raise prices in unison. Meanwhile the big-box retail customers had been demanding price decreases (and getting them from some of Midwest Tool's competitors). It wasn't clear the company needed all four manufacturing plants anymore. Sales were flat, and earnings before interest, taxes, depreciation, and amortization (EBITDA) steadily declined.

When I met Jim, he was a gray-haired, red-faced, teeth-clenching type of guy who looked like a walking heart attack in a monogrammed shirt. The bank, seeing its collateral disappearing, was beginning to make noise about the family putting up some personal guarantees. That wasn't Jim's only concern. His wife wanted him to spend more time with her at their condo in Florida, but he didn't dare leave the business because of constant "operational emergencies." Oh yes, Jim's sister Nora was lobbying for a dividend increase. When he asked what I thought the value range of the company was, I candidly answered $40 to $45 million.

Jim looked stricken. "That's what I thought," Jim whispered desperately, half to himself. "I will never be able to get out from under this thing."

"What thing?" I found myself whispering too, just as Jim was.

"It's obvious, isn't it?" Jim replied. "We rejected a $100 million offer, and I will never be able to hold my head up and agree to $40 million. We lost $60 million."

That's full-blown anchoring bias. Jim's frame of reference was calibrated wrong. He was anchored on a fantasy number that had never actually been offered. It was a work of fiction, a casual verbal indication at best, put on the table by a suitor attempting to romance and impress but who had little information or justification. Who knows if it ever would have closed?

But Jim had concluded that any number less than $100 million would represent a loss.

He could have thought about value very differently by setting a different anchor. He could have thought: *My Dad was incredible. He came to this country with nothing and created a business with a nationally known name employing hundreds of employees and an enterprise value of $40 million. What a terrific legacy, and what a terrific wealth creation!* Instead he anchored on *Coulda, woulda, shoulda taken that $100 million, and I will never be able to get my personal freedom until I get back there.* Ugh. What a prison he had created in his mind. Jim was all alone in his decision making. He hadn't assembled a team, didn't seem to have the character strengths associated with attracting talent, and was opposed to incurring the professional fees that he assumed (again, without real knowledge) went along with expert outside advisors. So his framing was solitary, biased, and ultimately risky. He was a victim of anchoring bias.

It's All About the Striving

Owner-managers usually push the limits of whatever system they are faced with, and I have the scars to prove it. The force of evolution is one of the most powerful explanations for behavior that researchers have found. It is a fundamental law of nature that, to evolve, one must push the limits, face hard challenges, and overcome personal adversity in order to grow strong and build personal resilience. Only by encountering the pain of failure, and after many tries overcoming it, can you build the strength of self-efficacy. In the framework of positive psychology, we say our subjective well-being is not optimized by achieving goals but by striving for them. What are the roles that owner-managers must employ to strive for their goals? What hats must they wear?

Read on.

2

Four Hats, One Head,
Big Challenge

> Where there are no alternatives, a wise
> man said, there are no problems.
> —WILLIAM F. BUCKLEY

MOST OWNER-MANAGERS REACH A POINT WHERE THEY DESCRIBE to me a significant discrepancy between where they are *now* with their enterprises and their lives compared to where they really *want to be*. My approach is to respectfully listen to them with a real desire to understand their perspective. I find that my acceptance of their situation as it truly is—in reality, right now—sets them free to change it if they really want to.

The responsibility for change and moving closer to your goals is left with you, the owner-manager. This is where I believe it lies—where it must lie. You, my client, are always free to take counsel or not. My approach is that the client always presents the reason for a capital gain transaction someday and helps me to understand the "whys." If you conclude that a value-capturing transaction gets you closer to your personal goals, then my colleagues and I are expert at that.

Very often, the discrepancy between the "where I am now" and the "where I would like to be" has something to do with the role you have played, are now playing, or would like to play—and some tension among them. So it's valuable to understand that the owner-manager plays four main roles: CEO, owner, family member, individual.

In this chapter, I will make some observations, which are necessarily in general and in the aggregate, about these roles. The fact that there are four roles indicates that the owner-manager of a privately held business does not have it easy. (See the illustration of these roles in Figure 2.1.) All four roles are big ones, each requires different skills, and they often have conflicting goals. How the owner-manager plays these roles has a powerful effect on enterprise value.

One Role Dominated at Eastern Machine Company

Let's look at how the roles specifically emerged over time for Don Lane, CEO of Eastern Machine Company (EMCo), a 300-employee organization that made precision parts for aerospace, defense, oil and gas, and technology industry applications.

When I met Don and his wife, Rose, they were in their early eighties, and I found them to be two of the most authentically kind and generous people anyone could imagine. They had all the characteristics of the entrepreneur owner-managers discussed in Chapter 1 with an extra supply of authenticity and fairness. Originally from Indiana, they had moved to New York in the 1950s and acquired a small machine shop. Don was trained in business, not as a machinist, but he was bright, a quick wit, and a technical tinkerer who appreciated what technology was allowing the company to do.

FIGURE 2.1 Community of Expert Advisors

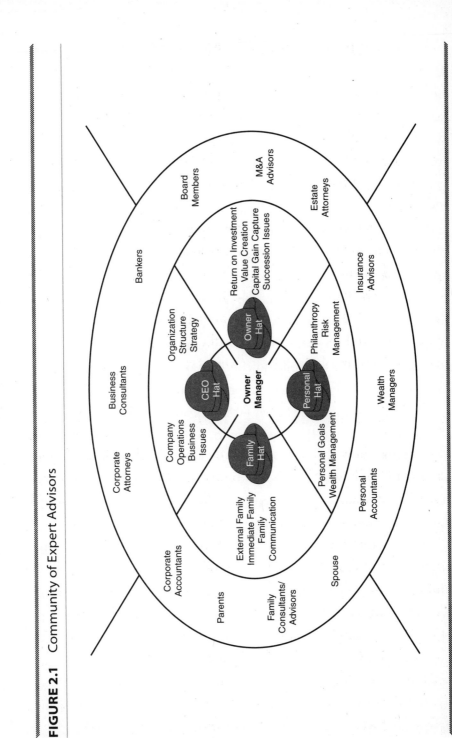

Over the course of 40 years, with Rose's support, Don built EMCo into a high-quality job shop. The couple's two sons had both joined the business after graduating from college, and they were struggling to pilot the company along. A complex business was becoming even more so, with tough decisions needing to be made on a number of issues: choice of which vertical markets to target, pricing, long-term contracts, acquisition of multimillion-dollar computer-controlled machine tools, and more. It took everything the family members had just to manage the day-to-day operations.

Although the Lanes were the majority stockholders, they didn't spend a lot of their time thinking in the owner's mode. They rarely had time or inclination to ask the questions that owners ask: "How are we doing with this investment? How is our return on investment? How are the decisions we are making as 'managers'—for example, taking on that oilfield contract, or putting that addition on the building—affecting the enterprise value for us as owners?"

As sometimes happens with family businesses, the industry was changing faster than the family could. The Lanes put their noses to the grindstone with typical entrepreneurial grit. But although all of them were working as hard as they could as managers, they were also bumping into the complications involved with being members of the family. The sons found it awkward to evaluate the performance of employees their father had hired and trained. They found it very difficult to reach consensus on developing a new business model even though the traditional approach was performing poorly. And one son, the director of operations, was quite certain he could not trust the numbers of the CFO (his brother).

The pressures, difficulties, and tensions in playing the roles of executives, owners, and family members were such that the Lanes rarely had the luxury of thinking about what they wanted for themselves individually, in the short term or the long term.

Role 1: Wearing the CEO Hat

The Lanes were experiencing what virtually all owner-managers do. They were assuming too many responsibilities—wearing too many hats (see Figure 2.1)—and it was becoming a burden. As an owner-manager you will find that the role of CEO or executive or senior manager of the company consumes most of your time—as much as 95 percent of it. When you're wearing this hat, you are acting as an agent for the owners (the stockholders) who have their capital, their reputation, and their legacy all wrapped up—and at risk—in the company. Sometimes the owners and managers are the same people, sometimes not.

When wearing the manager's hat, you are thinking about execution and operations: *How do I take the strategy and translate it into measurable goals and day-to-day behavioral change by my employees?* Your time frames are necessarily short—certainly shorter than the owners'—because the world's measuring times for managers are shorter. *What are my customers telling me about their needs and desires? How do I coach my salespeople to help communicate and position that information? What are the technology changes in our marketing channel, and how are we going to migrate from the old systems that we're all so comfortable with to access the newer, faster, cheaper, better technology that we all will have to spend time learning?*

With your manager's hat on, you are sweating out the working capital expansion and capital expenditure budget that results in positive cash flow . . . or not. The performance metrics for managers are well known.

The nature of the CEO's role can change significantly during the life of the enterprise, and that is often what motivates owner-managers to want a change of ownership. This is especially true when the duties of the CEO are no longer directly connected to the manager's ability or original passion. At that point the owner-manager finds herself spending less and less time on her unique competence, and frequently she wants out.

This is exactly what was happening at EMCo. The company suffered a string of tough years and survived a near-death experience (which required borrowing $20 million from a bank personally guaranteed jointly and severally by the entire family). But it was blessed to have a skilled board of advisors, a group of savvy CEOs of other successful manufacturing companies. After EMCo was out of the financial intensive care unit, the family and the board both recognized that something had to change, and together they agreed that bringing in an outsider as CEO was necessary. It was a huge emotional step—from a "family business" to a business that is owned by family members.

That's when Don and Rose ultimately began to act like owners interested in the long-term viability of the business. They listened to their advisors and agreed to bring on an experienced, nonfamily CEO. That changed everything.

Role 2: Wearing the Owner's Hat

Like the Lanes, most owner-managers typically will not spend much time in the owner role (maybe 5 percent). As an owner, you most likely will not either, but the decisions you make, while few in number and not very frequent, will usually be more impactful and can have a greater positive effect on enterprise value than the decisions made by managers. Think of it this way: *managers work* in *the business, but owners work* on *the business.*

In the owner's role, you are a principal in the business and your capital is at risk. You're thinking about the future strategy of the business, the allocation of resources (people, cash, time, technology, and so on) to support the strategy, the correct amount of invest-ment, and the return on investment in the short and long term. As a principal you are subject to those cognitive decision-making biases mentioned in the last chapter.

At the same time, you now feel responsible (obligated?) for the many employees you have, as well as their families who count on the sustained success of your business. Inwardly, you might think: *When I bought this company from the seller's estate, I didn't realize it came equipped with so many responsibilities.* A performance metric for owners might be, "Are the goals I am setting, and the resources I am allocating, positively impacting enterprise value? Will I eventually—someday—be able to achieve a return on my owner-ship investment?"

The Lanes were finally able to devote more time to answering these questions when they were able to convince a friend, Keith Maholz, a recently retired CEO of a large successful manufacturing company nearby, to take on the CEO role as a short-term assign-ment. Change came fast. The first thing Keith did was to redefine the strategy of the business. In so doing, he needed to review the cus-tomer base. When Keith looked into EMCo's largest, most revered, and longest-standing customer, he found something troubling. EMCo was losing about 33 percent on each order it delivered to that customer.

Keith asked why the family had allowed this to go on. The answer: The customer contributed to overhead. Hmm. "With cus-tomers like that, who needs competitors?" Keith commented. Soon, the large, money-losing customer was gone. Keith began to reorient EMCo toward higher-profit customers within faster-growing sec-tors, specifically defense. The company strengthened its capabilities to deliver precision prototypes and finished components much more rapidly than ever before.

By repositioning the company in markets where it was highly valued, as well as divesting customers and business that didn't fit for strategic or performance reasons—things the Lanes had been unable to do or even consider doing—EMCo's financial performance first turned up, then skyrocketed. EMCo was finally earning the high profits it deserved from building its highly engineered products. Keith had delivered the company to a decision point. He knew he didn't want to lead the business forever (remember, he had already retired once!) and the family knew they weren't the right-fit people to continue to lead what Keith had initiated so successfully.

That's when the Lanes began to think more broadly about the roles the family members should play in the business.

Role 3: Wearing the Family Member Hat

Here is where the Human (rather than the Econ) really shows up, and it is also this role that engenders a lot of conflicting emotions. As mentioned, the owner-manager is frequently a member of a business family, often a large and extended one. What's more, as with EMCo and the Lane clan, there may be other family members directly involved in the business—sometimes many of them—affected by the business. The family role can be central when it comes to the transaction, because as owner-manager you will consider the impact of a change on many parties who have financial and emotional stakes in the company.

The mental argument that goes on in the mind of the owner-manager who is also a family member often goes something like this:

> Originally (before I acquired it), this was my granddad's business, and I don't want to be the one to mess it up. We really ought to be considering that $25 million acquisition in Michigan, but if I bet equity on it, I could be

ing enough time with
my kids. Even when we're together, I'm constantly responding to e-mails and
texts from the sales force who are in multiple time zones.

Don and Rose Lane finally realized that it wasn't enough to bring
in a new CEO and spend more time thinking like owners. They also
had to think about the roles that the family members could play and
most wanted to play. These roles were not clear, and Don and Rose
didn't know how to approach clarifying them.

That's when Bigelow got the call. Over a period of several months,
my colleagues and I talked with Don, Rose, their children, and the
nonowner management team about "what the business needs" versus "what the owners want to do." Working in collaboration with
Keith and his management team, we urged that they continue to
reposition EMCo from its origins as a general machine shop to a
mission-critical defense contractor. We worked to identify the drivers
of enterprise value in the industry and target specific performance
metrics that aligned with how several potential strategic investors
reported their own performance.

During those discussions, we also identified which family employees would transition to the next ownership structure, and which
wouldn't. We were able to demonstrate to the family that it was in
their best interest to make certain that the go-forward managers had
ownership (or the economic value of ownership) in the company,
which would enable them to carry it into the new company with the
new investors. The Lanes, always fair, agreed.

gation Aunt Nancy's distribution, which she really needs to live on.
But, hey, now that I think about it, who guaranteed Aunt Nancy that distribution? Not me! And now my wife's loser brother wants a job and seems to
feel that because we are in the same family he is entitled to employment in
the so-called family business (for which I paid cash to become the majority
owner). Of course, there's no one I can talk to about all this. My family still
treats me like I'm a spacey teenager. I get no respect! I feel dissatisfied, even
angry. On top of all that, I feel guilt that I'm not spend

When we finally went to the private transaction market, we had a spectrum of highly attractive alternatives, from an offshore publicly owned strategic acquirer to a host of the best private equity groups in the world. Ultimately, the company was recapitalized by one of the best-fit private equity groups, an operations-oriented firm led by senior experienced people with manufacturing and operations backgrounds. EMCo became a strong platform for the private equity group and began to grow through acquisitions in the defense and aerospace domain. Keith Maholz found that he was having a lot of fun as CEO and decided to postpone his (second) retirement for a few years. Don and Rose are living it up in Florida with as much zest as they ran their business. The family shareholders made the tough strategic decisions that added up to a higher enterprise value, which included changing their own roles within the enterprise.

Role 4: Wearing the Individual Hat

Which brings me to the final role you play: as individual. Although your life as owner-manager is largely consumed by the business, you may not take into account your personal needs and wants in the transaction until the process actually begins.

Then a very different monologue plays out in your head:

> One of my goals has always been to get really fit. I have also been intending to engage a professional wealth manager to work on a detailed financial planning document for my wife and me. I also want to make sure we get more vacation time, starting with that summer trip to the Rockies we've always talked about. I also have some personal development goals I have been putting off and I want to find some time to spend on them.

It's amazing but true that owner-managers often put themselves— their individual wants and desires—last. That truth is so contrary to the popular stereotype of the self-absorbed, me-first entrepreneur.

George Gallagher Illuminates the Roles

George Gallagher, the president of Gallagher Companies, had long struggled with the roles he had been playing at the company that his great-grandfather had founded in 1888 in Ireland. Gallagher Companies designed and manufactured the most aesthetically beautiful furniture in the world, and it had products in Versailles, the White House, the Louvre, and the Vatican. It is regarded as one of the world's most innovative companies in the high-end furniture business and has all of the industry awards and the customer list to prove it.

George was torn among at least three of four roles. He had reached the point in the business when he'd begun to assess the future leadership needs of the company, and he had come to the conclusion that he was no longer suited to the CEO role. The bad parts were beginning to feel much worse than the good parts felt good. There was big-time negativity bias.

"It's like this," he said. "If you need someone who can sketch the beautifully proportioned arc of the arm of a Queen Anne chair and solve its design and manufacturing issues, I am your man. If, on the other hand, you want to discuss how we are going to deal with reducing the number of stock-keeping units by consolidating our parts inventory—honestly, that bores me. I have no interest in that."

This disinterest in the CEO role—a disdain for professional "management"—was a real worry for George. "As the owner of the business, I want the CEO to deal with that stuff. But as the CEO, I just don't want to—I am not turned on by solving those kinds of problems. They're not my unique competence, although I acknowledge they must be solved. And ultimately, if I allow that tension to continue, I'm not acting responsibly for the business."

Dealing with the managerial and ownership issues had implications for his family. "Look," George said, "my 88-year-old mother is dependent on the business for her livelihood. She has strong opinions about how the business should be operated and how the management changes we are making affect the legacy of the business. Not to mention my sister, Connie, whom I am very close to—both as a family member and business advisor—and who is instrumental in new product development. My sister's husband, Bruce, is a particularly skilled international sales guy who is willing to make three- to four-week global forays into developing markets. He has built important relationships in Asia, which are essential to our continued growth and success. So for us, a long Thanksgiving weekend at my mom's home in the mountains—given our intertwined business and family relationships—can be a very complex and stressful gathering."

Not surprisingly, the family members were all of different minds about what George should do and how a transaction might be handled. His mother understood George's desire to take the next step, but she was worried about her own security if he left the company completely. George's sister thought he should follow his instincts. Bruce, the brother-in-law, assured George that he would be there to take on more responsibility, if that made sense.

George concluded that his CEO role did not align with his owner's role and that his role as family member was coloring everything else. There was a very real and observable conflict between "what the business needs" and "what the owner wants to do." Just to add to the complexity, his individual wants were somewhere else altogether. "I really am called to spend more time with the homeless medical clinic we just started," he told me, "and I have just pledged over $5 million in personal capital to it. But it needs more energy from me right now, more than it needs additional money. The organization needs direction and passion that it seems only I can provide. Connie feels that the stock we have from our father was a 'gift' and we should act like it was. I acknowledge his generosity, but darn it, I added value to this enterprise over 30 years of my working life too."

The dilemma George faced is not uncommon among owner-managers. But few have the strength to face up to the needs of the organization and pursue their own passions. George did. He changed his title from CEO to Interim CEO—which reassured his mother that he would not do anything rash that might jeopardize her security. He then took the first step in working toward an eventual transition for the company: he began to assemble an expert advisory team to help him prepare for the transaction—which included his brother-in-law Bruce, whom the family trusted. George had recognized that the role of CEO was no longer viable for him and that he had to start thinking more like an owner *and* take into account his own personal desires. Within three years, George Gallagher had realized a significant capital gain, a new CEO had taken over his position, and the wants and needs of the family members had all been considered and met.

For George, good felt good again.

Assembling the Core Advisory Team

Because wearing four hats is so difficult, the demands so onerous and often contradictory, and the workload so intense, the best owner-managers—the ones who want to have a wealth creation event someday—do not wait until the day before they engage an M&A advisor to assemble a team of world-class advisors. Many studies have shown that expert teams are very much more effective when they have worked together over a period of time or repeatedly. So when it comes time to consider a $50 million–plus capital gain event, it's essential for you to have a team of world-class advisors by your side and on your side. You can be certain that the potential investors looking at you across the negotiating table will have theirs.

The following are some of the most important members of the team.

Transaction Special Legal Counsel

You no doubt already have an attorney as a general corporate legal counsel, and chances are good that he or she has earned your confidence. But a capital gain transaction is different than everyday legal matters that are handled by general counsel. Every investor, regardless of asset class, who is thinking of making a $50 million–plus investment will have a world-class M&A specialty attorney who has done hundreds of transactions, many of them in the last couple of years. You need specialized legal talent of similar caliber. Many of my clients engage an M&A special counsel to serve as "temporary help" during the planning and execution of a wealth creation transaction. The benefit of the special counsel, in addition to his experience and skills, is that he will be intimately familiar with what "market" currently means when it comes to legal terms and conditions. Your counsel will draft a stock purchase agreement that is the first draft the investor sees. If counsel has some months or years ahead of the transaction to get to know you and your personal and professional goals, it stands to reason that he will be able to advise you more effectively. Typically special legal counsel supplements, but doesn't replace, your existing general counsel.

Estate Attorney

A specialist trust and estate attorney who will think through your long-term goals and how to provide for them in your estate is another invaluable member of the team. For example, an owner-manager who is looking forward to a future capital gain transaction might be advised by a trust and estate attorney to move some of the ownership outside of her estate at some point during the process of building enterprise value. That way, when the value is finally captured in a capital gain, some of that gain can be available to fund other commitments the owner-manager has deemed to be important—for example, family trusts or philanthropic causes. When the estate attorney knows you and your family, even a bit, she can provide better input on an estate plan.

Wealth Advisor

When I recommend adding a wealth advisor to the advisory team, many owner-managers get uncomfortable. This is complicated territory, both intellectually and emotionally, because so many seasoned, successful entrepreneurs feel strongly (for better or worse) about wealth advisors. Most have experience with them, some of it far from happy.

A curious thing happens in a wealth creation transaction. Before the transaction, most owner-managers have few liquid assets, and the vast majority of their assets are in the highly concentrated, illiquid, risky ownership of their private business that they were controlling and building. Their "hands-on" energy and efforts usually build enterprise value. Then they go through a wealth creation transaction, and now their balance sheet goes upside down. Suddenly they have the bulk of their wealth in cash and are bewildered about where to invest it to *preserve* it. (They already have earned their fortune, right?) They often are swiftly surrounded by a gaggle of new acquaintances—seemingly sophisticated wealth advisors and brokers talking about complex financial products. Some of these new best friends seem a tiny bit more interested in trying to sell what they have rather than listening to what the newly wealthy individuals need or want. Please don't misunderstand: I have many wealth advisor friends whose ability I have high regard for; there are some outstanding ones who merit your trust. We will focus much more deeply on this topic in Chapter 6. But let me ask this now: why wait to interview some wealth advisors to see whom you like, whose style you are comfortable with, whether you prefer a large logo legacy firm or a smaller independent boutique?

Merger and Acquisition Advisor

This is the domain where I spend most of my time. Not all types of M&A advisors are the same, nor are all advisors of the same type equal. There is prodigious inconsistency in levels of experience, technical competence, and (possibly most important to you) empathic understanding of the needs of owner-managers. Many highly trained advisors assume that, just as in math class, there is only one right answer to the problem. They may not have cultivated active listening skills. They may not have sufficient patience to take into account the uniqueness of each client situation. And it is highly likely they don't believe, as I do, that "not everything that counts can be counted."

M&A advisors are different in many ways—for example, the strategies they employ in working with clients, the expertise of their client teams, their transaction execution skills, their philosophies, and organizational cultures. Many are what I would call "process driven," which means they execute the same methodology for every transaction, check all the necessary boxes, and hope for the best.

Generally for these firms, at one end of the spectrum there are the logo/legacy "full-service financial institutions" and at the other the independently owned boutiques. The logo/legacy firms are filled with lots of really bright, elite, and highly educated people. Many, maybe even most, of those professionals are better acquainted with the relatively transparent public market than they are with the inefficient, opaque private company transaction market where owner-managers play. Many firms, both large and small, are owned by large diversified financial institutions. They can be highly transaction driven and take on a large number of engagements with the expectation of closing some of them.

Many of these large firms have organized into industry-specialized groups, which enables them to leverage their less-experienced junior staff. Of course, these industry groupings are theoretical constructs, because no industry is so perfectly defined, nor is any company so completely engaged in one industry. There is benefit for the expert who works within the industry group, because he doesn't have to think particularly long and deeply about the client's company. Because he knows the industry terrain so well, he doesn't think it necessary to consider the effects of a wide range of possibilities. If he has deep industry expertise, he often has a static view of how things will (should) go together. He also has many potential conflicts. Industry specialists by definition are unable to apply patterns of knowledge learned in one industry to different situations and come up with new solutions. Creativity is dampened. Innovative thinking is discouraged. I am allergic to this kind of behavior, which I view as putting what is convenient for the advisor ahead of the clients' interest.

In addition to size, there are other distinctions among M&A advisors. Some are "finders" who work for acquirers on the buy side. Some are "business brokers" who, just as a real estate agent does, take listings of businesses for sale. And there are FINRA registered broker-dealers. The Financial Industry Regulatory Authority (FINRA), previously called the NASD, is the association that regulates financial intermediaries. A firm that is a registered broker-dealer has committed to investing in and complying with the highest ethical and legal standards. Gaining this classification requires a registration and audit of the firm's capital and its financial statements. The firm's client-facing people are required to be individually licensed and proficient in the domains in which they work. Compliance reporting is strict. I cannot imagine why any seasoned, successful owner-manager would dream of engaging an M&A advisor that is not FINRA registered.

So how to choose? If one accepts that, in this digital age, firms and groups of firms are approximately equal to one another in access to information, communications technology, sophisticated analytical tools, and regulatory compliance, then one can expect that the differential in outcomes for clients between firms is determined by other factors. A crucial one is the depth of the social intelligence of each group—the ability to read the emotions of others (empathy), to gauge the intentions of people, and to excel in the ability to gain trust and build powerful relationships. Social intelligence in advisors is always in great demand. This is particularly true because of the unique nature of entrepreneur owner-manager clients. As you have seen, when they are compared with others—nonbusiness owner-managers, for example—they have far more at stake. A sharp, well-honed sense of empathy makes an enormous difference, and with it an ability to exercise judgment, to gain cooperation, and to persuade. To put the matter as simply as possible, it pays to be socially smart in the M&A advisory business.

Social intelligence is multiplied in a team. I believe that a small, socially intelligent team has a distinct advantage over another type of advisor who is also active in the private transaction market: the skilled, solitary individual. At Bigelow when the team kicks off an engagement with a new client, we usually employ a "swarm strategy" in which we deploy a number of experienced members with unique skills and different strengths. Some team members research, screen, and begin preliminary dialogues with potential investors; others go about researching and drafting industry and company information. Then the team converges on a client's information, offering insights, seeing different patterns among potential investor types, and suggesting time compression strategies. A team working in this way has advantages over the individual, even if that person has high social intelligence. Solitary advisors can either seek investors or analyze industry and company data; they can't do both at the same time.

By utilizing a socially intelligent, unique team, the company has the ability to apply the team resources that have the best fit for the client situation or technical issue at hand. The team members together also have a capability that is exponentially more powerful than the individuals would have alone, because those team members are constantly learning and growing—in complementary domains— from one another.

Lastly and perhaps most important, I wouldn't pay much attention to the websites and descriptive brochures of advisor firms. I would insist on speaking directly with a few past clients to get their objective and candid insight on the firm, the engagement leader, the outcome, and the style with which the engagement was handled. Was it a positive, energy-creating experience? Did the clients have any fun? Are they happy with the outcome? Knowing what they know now, would they use the same firm (and team) again? You're the captain of the ship, and you are trying to find a great navigator to help you through the shoals and reefs of the private company transaction market. Talk to someone who has successfully used that same navigator before.

Advisory Board

Not all clients have advisory boards, but most of the best ones do. Being an owner-manager is, by definition, a lonely place. You "think different," right? Usually there are few trusted peers you can confide in about the business. If you haven't built a significant enterprise before, now is the time to start—every day is a new day. You can read Jim Collins until you are blue in the face but there is nothing like a battle-scarred CEO as a member of your advisory board. He's done it before. He has the scars to prove it. He can tell stories that you will find illuminating. Then there is the wealth of resources and contacts that good advisory board members will bring to the party. Because all of the members are already successful and are giving advice that has long-term effect, the most productive boards frequently use compensation for members in equity, or in a way that economically mimics equity, so their economic outcome is aligned with yours.

The Arc of the Enterprise and the Entrepreneur

The development of a privately owned enterprise travels along an arc (sometimes it may feel more like a jagged series of steps than a smooth arc) characterized by inflection points that are systematic and predictable (see Figure 2.2). The decisions the owner-manager makes at each point along the way (decisions that are often influenced by the multiple hats he wears and how she or he perceives the roles will be affected) determine the ability of the business to achieve its optimal performance, create the greatest enterprise value, generate the largest number of attractive opportunities for a transaction someday, and result in positive legacy—when and if that day arrives.

So let us travel along the arc and consider some of the decisions that affect enterprise value at the various inflection points along the way.

Starting Out

Most of the best-seasoned successful entrepreneur owner-managers I have met have a superior skill, possibly even a distinctive skill in one of two domains. The majority of the hundreds of the best ones

FIGURE 2.2 The Life Arc of an Entrepreneur Owner-Manager

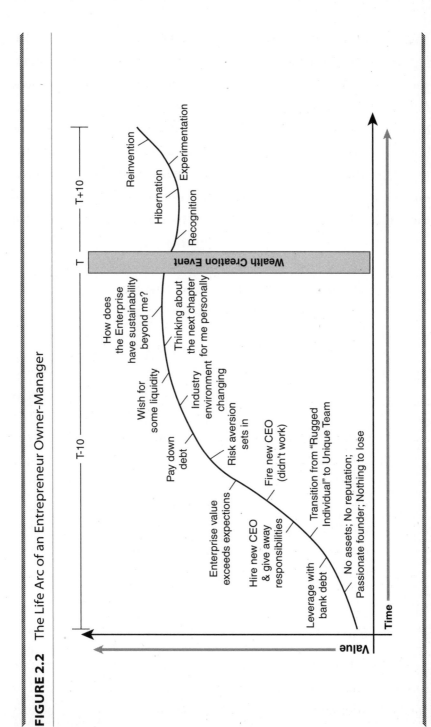

I know have a distinct competence in the domain of sales and selling. The second significant, but much smaller, percentage of EOMs have distinctive capability in a technical domain; they are experts of some kind. They might be true technology protégés or just innovative tinkerers who understand the business so intimately they can innovate new ways of solving technical problems.

Whatever it is they start with, these rugged individuals learn their management skills along the way, and you'd give them a good belly laugh if you suggested they are engaged in what Peter Drucker called "the science of management." Most of them simply do not have the interest, expertise, experience, relevant education, or discipline working "in the business" in their roles as managers to make executive decisions that are consistently and scientifically about building enterprise value.

The owner-manager whose primary management skill is selling comes at the business with a very distinct understanding of what *selling* means. While some people may disparage the selling skill as pressure tactics or spin, everybody knows that nothing happens without making a sale of a product or service. For the typical owner-manager, however, the approach to selling is very different from that of the owner-manager who has spent time in a large corporate environment. The former type tends to be obsessed with delighting customers and creating over-the-top experiences for them. The best owner-managers I know go at the business in a fundamental way. They find a real niche for their product or service, connect with customers who fervently want that product, and deliver it well. They are energetic, persuasive, and professionally persistent; they have grit. More often than not, they close the sale and keep their customers for a long time.

The second type of owner as manager, the technical tinkerer, may have formal education, sometimes a technology degree, but in most cases he will not. Either way, he is able to develop and deliver a product or service that is so clearly technically superior to the competition's that it sets the standard for the customer. Even major company customers will source products and services from small suppliers if they are technically superior to those of the competition and if their performance metrics prove it.

As we have discussed, in the owner role, the owner-manager is possessed of distinct character strengths (authenticity, leadership, fairness, gratitude, and zest) that, in combination, give him or her an "attracting" personality. This aids in selling and in enabling that owner-manager to attract and retain teams of talented people.

But, at the early stage of the arc of the enterprise, owner-managers are usually doing much more than just selling or pursuing their technical expertise. They are usually the "chief cook and bottle washer," doing whatever it takes, for as long as it takes, to make the company cash positive. Even as other members of the team come on board with more clearly defined functional roles (for example, operations, controller, and sales), the owner-manager continues to happily and energetically skip among all roles . . . *but is almost always the chief seller*.

In that sales role, and at a period when the company is likely to be very much in need of a steady stream of sales, it is understandable that the owner-manager may sometimes make a decision that looks good in the short term but does not necessarily build enterprise value.

Take Jeff Hastings, the entrepreneur owner-manager of Victory Windows. Jeff had decided to build a relationship with the big-box home center, offering installation services for the windows the customer purchased there. It was a clever model for both businesses, and seamless to the customer. All you had to do was show up at the retailer, select your windows, opt for installation, and pay with your credit card at the checkout station. Victory Windows would call you and then schedule the installation at your site, and all of the paperwork would be taken care of by the home center.

The model was very seductive for Jeff. He did not have to build or maintain a sales force; he had only to deal with the retailer, not with direct customers; and his sales rose as the retailer's rose. Unfortunately, it was a business model that had no possibility for a capital gain someday. Why? It's obvious, isn't it? No investor or senior debt provider would consider the recapitalization or acquisition of Victory Windows because the customer concentration risk was far too high. Jeff was always at the mercy of the home center, which might switch installers at any time. As a result, Jeff finally concluded he should optimize and distribute all of the cash he had each year. Incredibly, he was in the squeeze where sales with that customer were increasing well but had no positive effect on enterprise value.

Borrowing

In almost all cases, entrepreneur owner-managers capitalize their businesses with equity and also with bank debt, allowing the business to grow faster, to add more capabilities, or both. The business is the technical "borrower," but only in conjunction with its owner-manager. Owner-managed businesses are almost always required to provide a personal guarantee of the majority stockholder (and frequently that person's spouse) to the lender. The personal guarantee is in addition to the normal lien the bank holds on the assets of the business. (Banks do not require personal guarantees from public companies, or even from larger private companies with a more diverse stockholder group.) Banks clearly think you need to have some "skin in the game"—not merely that you lose upside, but that you will lose personal assets to the extent of the unpaid bank loan if things go south.

Not surprisingly, the decision to borrow has an important and sometimes inhibiting effect on the owner-manager. If you as EOM cannot pay back the loan on the bank's terms, the bank can take possession of your business and personal assets. It can take your house, clean out your bank accounts, raid your portfolio, or do whatever it takes to pay down the loan balance. While living under the bank's thumb in this way, it can often be difficult for the owner-manager to execute as boldly on the plan as she might like. Not surprisingly, my colleagues and I have found that as businesses mature and grow in value, removing the personal guarantee from the senior debt is often a very positive thing to do for the future sustainability of the business. It gives the owner-manager a sigh of relief that the business is mature enough to stand on its own—and often unlocks an acceleration in the business plan.

Building a Team

Once the enterprise is up and running, most owner-managers come to the uncomfortable realization that the company's growth depends on attracting and retaining a leadership team of skilled people who share the purposes and goals of the owner-manager. (This is distinct from the core advisory team.) To do this, the EOM almost always has to look for talent outside the company; naturally, some of these hires will work out, but, painfully, many will not. The hiring decisions, however, have tremendous significance on enterprise value, because the qualities and abilities of the management team become critically important during the company transition.

The transition from competent individual doing it all to becoming the builder and leader of a team is one of the most difficult challenges facing most business owners. Many owner-managers, even once they have a capable team in place, have a hard time letting go of unilateral decision making about almost everything, especially strategy. For team members to be effective, however, they have to help develop, understand, and agree with the strategy. They have to be provided with the resources needed to implement the strategy, and they need clear measurements so they know how success (or lack of it) is being measured. Most owner-managers eventually accept that these things are essentials.

Ann Farrell Builds a Team

Let me illustrate the journey so far with the story of Ann Farrell and her printing company. Ann was of the dominant owner-manager variety: she was a great seller, although she didn't need much help on the technical side of the equation either. Ann started out as the main (and only) salesperson for the printing company her father had founded a generation earlier. Over a period of 20 years, she grew the business to over $40 million in sales and above-average industry profitability. Ann's sales success was based not solely on her ability to cajole and persuade: she and her team had developed a differentiated printed product that enabled customers to save, on average, 10 percent on the total invoice. That delighted customers, because it gave them the option to invest the savings in something else or, as they often did, order 10 percent more of the printed materials that Ann's company produced.

Although Ann's talents as an advocate for her company's printing prowess had played a major role in building the company, she also had a lot of help. For her, when the time for hiring came along, she did not experience it as a bump in the road. In fact, she discovered she had a gift as a management team builder. The first two members to join her team became especially valued colleagues. One was a talented and experienced printing plant manager; the other a homegrown controller. Although neither of them had much in the way of formal education, either one would usually be the smartest person in almost any room. They were exceptionally bright, quick learners, thankful for the opportunity Ann was giving them and unfailingly loyal to her. Together, they gradually filled in the team with about 15 more midlevel managers. These others too played pivotal roles, but they were not privy to as much information about company performance as the top three executives shared with one another.

This would later prove to be an issue that Ann had to deal with forthrightly.

Becoming General Manager

Like Ann, most owner-managers find great satisfaction in the pursuit of running an owner-managed business—relying on no one else to make the sale, rally the troops, or lead the business. They relish the ultimate individual challenge: "You only eat what you kill."

Gradually, however, as a company moves along the arc, the owner-manager is increasingly called upon to attend to the tasks of the general manager—tasks she or he often disdains or finds frustrating. In the early days, the leadership team can have informal and ad hoc get-togethers standing around the coffee maker. Now the meetings have to be scheduled and take place in a conference room. Because you, the owner-manager (who are still the CEO), spend more and more time managing the organization, you are less and less able to put your superior ability—selling—to use. You intend to pay a call on some of the old customers or visit some of the new ones with the sales team, but you have to meet with, say, the healthcare insurer. Or the manufacturing engineers want to talk to you about a new cost-saving device in the plant. Perhaps human resources has planned a kickoff event for the employee wellness program and you really should be there to say a few words. Maybe the latest cost estimate on the new project needs your approval.

You get my point. But hear me on this: one of the saddest, most predictable, and most discouraging phenomena I have seen *repeatedly* in owner-managed companies is the owner-manager beginning to use his superior ability less and less because he feels he has to spend more time being the manager, the president, or whatever the title may be. As a result, he feels less and less energized, less powerful, and less happy. Someday he wakes up and thinks, *Wait, I think I can hire someone to do this for me.* This is especially trying, because owner-managers are fundamentally wary of the CEO species—unless and until they find the right person.

The next inflection point on the arc: hiring a new CEO.

Hiring a CEO

In my own experience as a private company owner-manager, I have hired a fair number of people at all levels in the company over a period of 30 years. I would say that we got our hiring decisions right about a third of the time. The results of an informal poll of friends and colleagues show that I am not alone in this fairly unimpressive record. Not only did we get a lot of hires wrong, we often didn't manage the employment very well. Frequently we held onto people too long, even after we knew they were not a good fit. (You probably never did that.)

You might expect that the hiring percentage for a CEO would be better, but I don't think it is. In fact, even fewer of them may end up being a good fit. Part of the reason for this is that the new CEO brings such enormous change to the role of the owner-manager that it poses a tremendous challenge.

The new CEO is expected to bring a clearer and more functional structure to the organization. But as other roles become more distinct, your role as owner-manager becomes less so. The new CEO makes very specific job assignments for everyone else, but not for you. She introduces all kinds of systems—for tracking labor hours, inventory costs, and customer data. Outside consultants are engaged to develop and implement software implementation and to conduct team-building initiatives. Budgets are built up line by line, approved by multiple layers of managers, and then officially adopted and slavishly adhered to. Good-bye, impromptu meetings around the coffee maker. Hello, hierarchy.

Then comes the day when you are doing something you have always done, perhaps offering direct feedback to a salesperson, and the new CEO gives *you* grief: "You didn't go through proper channels. You should have spoken with his manager first!" What? You start to get the feeling this new CEO just doesn't get it. She's not simply changing processes and systems, she is messing around with the fundamental things that made the company great: values, relationships, and behaviors—*the way we do things*.

This can become such a volatile situation that it often explodes and lands you at the next point along the enterprise arc: firing the new CEO.

Growing Cautious

Whoever is serving as CEO, the next segment of the enterprise arc is an exciting one—you begin to string together a series of wins. Sales climb. EBITDA as a percentage of sales reaches two times the industry average. All signs are that your company is providing something of great value to your customers, something they are willing to pay a higher price for than anything your competitor has to offer.

During this period, as you're juggling your four roles, building your team, and adding capabilities, you begin to get the scary feeling—in bursts and flashes—that maybe, just maybe, your business model might achieve, maybe even exceed, what you thought it could when you got started. You wake up another morning at

4:00 a.m., and it suddenly hits you: *Holy X@#$, the value of the company is higher than I ever thought it would be! It might be worth $50 or $60 million.* And then another realization comes crashing in: outside of a couple of nice homes and some fancy cars, the vast majority of your wealth in this whole world is in your enterprise. And, a third, unsettling, thought creeps in: deep down in your heart of hearts you know you just aren't as close to the business as you used to be. Could you mess things up? If you do, enterprise value could start going in the other direction. *Gulp!*

Once you have this series of revelations, your attitude changes. And that becomes apparent to everyone. At the Monday morning management meeting (which you grudgingly agreed to convene and at which you've arrived 10 minutes late), the VP of engineering says he has some interesting news to report. It seems there's a young company, based in Denver, that has developed a game-changing technology for your industry. The VP met the owner at a cocktail reception at a recent conference, had some discussion, and he reckons the young Denver company is ripe to be acquired.

"How much?" you ask.

"Oh, in the $10 million range, I think," says the VP, as if it were nothing.

Before you had your revelations that might have sounded like an interesting proposition. Now, however, you think to yourself, *Are these guys nuts? Ten million bucks of my money? The company's only worth $50 or $60 million. I can't afford to risk losing that much of the value.*

Notice the anchoring bias that colors your thinking, even though the $60 million figure is your own invention and the $10 million number is pure speculation.

It gets worse. As enterprise value climbs and then exceeds an amount you never dared hope for (or at least you think it does), a curious thing happens to you. The risk of failure involved in executing the next step of the plan to increase enterprise value doesn't look worth the marginal addition to enterprise value it could bring. Suddenly—*click!*—a tumbler slides home and a door to an ancient part of your brain opens: *Whoa! I had better lock in the tremendous gain in enterprise value now, not worry about growing it any farther. It would be risky under any circumstances, but it's way too risky if it means I could lose a big chunk of the enterprise value I have built up.*

That's decision-making bias #2: loss aversion. It happens to you exactly as it eventually does to every EOM lucky enough to have built a lot of enterprise value—as it does to every business owner or investor at some point.

Boxed In: A Specific Instance of Loss Aversion

Let's consider loss aversion in light of a particular decision that many owner-managers have to make, one that will definitely have an effect on building enterprise value: how to deal with the big-box retail channel.

Over the past decade or so, as owner-managers have built their businesses they have had to deal with the proliferation of marketing and selling channels—wholesale, retail, catalogue, Internet, big-box, boutique, branded, private label, and others. This is known as "channel proliferation." A major driving force in the growth of some businesses over the last 10 years has been their decision to sell to—or concentrate on—customers in the big-box channel.

Some otherwise cautious EOMs have been seduced by the sheer volume and attractive growth rates of the big-box retail channel as customers for their businesses. At my company we have observed some EOMs who have been working for years to build volume in small independent customers and then become intoxicated by the thought of selling to one customer with thousands of stores. How simple that would be, right? How easily your company could double the volume of goods it sells, probably in six months to a year! What's more, big-box customers may make your company a better supplier, as they are demanding and focused, employ state-of-the-art distribution technology (and insist you do the same), are cost conscious, and are filled with the promise of greater and greater sales volume for your company's products.

So you go for it. At first, everything goes great. But over time, you find yourself making more and more key decisions, not with the hope of increasing revenue from the big-box customer, but from fear of losing it. As the customer comes to represent an ever-larger proportion of total sales, you find yourself agreeing to demands that you would never have met if the customer were a smaller one. You're dealing with product-line reviews that inevitably lead to price declines, enduring threats of taking the business offshore, having to make "contributions" to advertising, providing selling help in customer stores, providing consignment inventory, and ultimately, extending credit terms far beyond normal industry terms.

Then comes the kicker. The big-box customer, who is under consumer price pressure every bit as severe as the pressure it is putting on you, hires a big-name consulting firm that recommends some reengineering, and that inevitably entails reducing the number of suppliers the big box should work with. Agony? Yes. Surprised? You shouldn't be.

As Kahneman and Tversky, mentioned in Chapter 1, proved over 20 years ago, people willingly and consistently take on more risk to avoid a loss than they will to anticipate a gain. That will apply to you if, because of one key decision, you now find yourself with a single dominant customer, who dictates almost everything about your business: product, delivery, quality, price, terms, and conditions. That initial decision led to a multitude of related decisions.

You expanded your capacity and added fixed costs to accommodate the giant. You have almost no choice but to continue unhappily down the road, trying desperately to increase sales to other customers, only to capitulate to the (increasingly unreasonable) demands of the big-box customer again and again.

That decision, which seemed to promise growth and prosperity, actually sent enterprise value spiraling downward. Sorrow and woe ensue.

Complexity Creates Too Much Choice

There is no doubt that this kind of decision complexity will characterize the environment in which owner-managers will operate for the next hundred years, so you have to learn to deal with it.

As the enterprise continues to grow, and as it faces more and more decisions about more and more complex situations, a new challenge emerges: the "paradox of choice." This phenomenon is described by Barry Schwartz in his terrific volume *The Paradox of Choice* (2004). In it, he describes the psychological and economic foundation of the world of complexity that owner-managers live in. The developed world has gone from an economy of scarcity for them to an abundance of choice—about everything. And Schwartz provides empirical evidence that just facing choice is frequently stressful, resulting in increased anxiety, and curiously, an inability to choose at all—a hesitation to act. Too much choice appears to cause us to escalate our expectations; ruminate on opportunity costs (other choices); anticipate regret (of making the wrong choice); engage in analysis-paralysis, resulting in no decision; and ultimately blame ourselves for our pathetic inability to act, resulting in depression. Nobody wants a world with no choices, of course. But Schwartz argues that while moving from no choices to some choices is good, moving from some choices to a lot is a recipe for dissatisfaction.

That's exactly what happens for many owner-managers who are faced with more choices than they have ever had to deal with before: which channel to sell through, whom to hire or fire, how to structure the organization, which activities to pursue, how much debt to assume, what capital investments to make, which markets to enter or exit, what products to make or offer, and which partners to collaborate with.

The owner-manager begins to realize that every decision she makes will affect enterprise value. Risk aversion may take over; the owner-manager does not wish to jeopardize what she has built. If so, she may make less-than-optimal decisions such as embarking on diversifying endeavors that actually diffuse resources, confuse the company's identity, and destroy enterprise value.

Ann Farrell Opens the Books

Ann Farrell and her printing company team reached a point where it became very clear to me that the tyranny of choice had set in.

As the company grew larger, and as it purchased more and more equipment to meet demand—which required more and more borrowing, as each of the specialized printing presses cost over $10 million—it became clear that the three top team members could not make the choices without input from the larger group. But that would mean giving them greater access to the performance data, including detailed financials, in order for them to make the right operational decisions that would enable them to meet their financial targets. This ran counter to Ann's basic nature as a salesperson and second-generation company owner.

This is often the case with an enterprise at this stage of the arc. Some of the team members—often the best ones—will insist on financial transparency. They will argue they cannot be completely successful in their roles unless they have full knowledge of the company's performance in as much detail and depth as the owner-manager himself does. At this, I have seen many an owner-manager balk. Sharing details about strategy is one thing. Opening up the books for scrutiny is something else altogether. However, the owner-manager must bring his team inside. Without full knowledge of the financials, the team cannot make well-informed decisions and operate at their greatest potential. Without a strong and contributing team, the enterprise can never realize its full value.

Finally, after a number of sleepless nights, Ann came to the conclusion that the information had to be shared. Her experienced plant manager and trusted controller emphatically validated her decision. This realization proved to be a major inflection point for her and one that enabled the company to significantly build value.

Ann and I collaborated on how to present the financials to her people. She decided to call a meeting of her entire management team with the goal of sharing the necessary information, and she wanted me to be a part of the presentation. We convened in a windowless conference room just off the plant floor. I will never forget her anxiety in that room that afternoon. The printing presses were thundering away—boom, boom, boom—and the air was thick with the smell of printing ink and solvent. The management team shuffled in, managers in ties and shift supervisors in company smocks.

My role was to talk about and explain the income statement and, to do that, I had to start with some basic principles. "Let's begin with gross margin," I said. "That's the amount that's left after we pay all direct manufacturing expenses, including paper, ink, and direct labor." I went on to talk about selling, general, and administrative (SG&A) expenses, and, then, I got to EBITDA, the six cents on the dollar that went to facilities investment, bonuses, and cash distributions to the owners.

I paused to let the information sink in. After a moment, Buddy, a 50-something, overall-clad shift supervisor from the deep South raised his hand. I noticed, out of the corner of my eye, Ann grimacing. She had warned me that some of the managers might have questions about potentially sensitive items like owners' compensation.

But that was not what was perplexing Buddy. "You kiddin'?" he said. "Are you sayin' that even after we operate the plant workin' as hard as we can, 24 hours a day, 7 days a week, sweatin' our brains out in the hot plant, that for every dollar of sales we bring in, all we have left is an itty-bitty li'l' ol' six cents?"

"Yup. That's right, Buddy, six cents on every dollar of sales."

"*That's IT?*"

This was a revelation to all in the room. Ann looked as if she were developing a bad headache. I forged ahead. "Yup, that's it," I said. "But that doesn't *have* to be it." I explained that there were usually ways to improve EBITDA, and gave an example. "The industry data show that *this company's* paper waste percentage is about twice as high as that of the best printers in the world. If this company could equal their performance and cut the paper waste in half, it could bump that 6 cents up to 10. That would give a lot more to invest, to allocate in bonuses, and to distribute some profit. Now, I know this company may not be as good as some of the best printers in the world, but it could get better, couldn't it?"

That moment of information sharing was golden. The emotional temperature in the room changed. Metaphorically, everyone got on the same side of the table. Buddy and all the middle management team members recognized how difficult it had been for Ann to share the performance data with them, appreciated her authenticity and candor, and reacted positively. They took on the EBITDA challenge, and the results exceeded expectations. In less than a year, paper waste fell from 14 to 6 percent, and EBITDA climbed from 6 percent to 14 percent.

Ann had managed her way through an important phase of the company's life and had been willing to make a real change in her own behavior, and it made all the difference in creating enterprise value.

Taking on Too Much Responsibility and Too Many Obligations

Once the company is growing and the team is in place and operating successfully, often your days become more about playing defense than offense, more about preserving than growing. One day there are so many people in the plant that you don't know everyone's job, much less his or her name. You have a dawning realization that the increasing time commitment required to marginally increase enterprise value is feeling less and less like fun. There's a recognition that it is just good sense to lock in what appears to be a certain and large capital gain and put something less concentrated and more liquid in the bank. When that starts to happen, the interests of the owner-manager and the long-term potential of the business are beginning to diverge. (It becomes a case of what the business needs versus what the owners want.) It's definitely time to consider looking for the next majority owner who will sustain the business beyond your personal ownership of it.

The success of the enterprise also has an effect on the owner-manager personally. He may take on too many responsibilities, not just at the company, but in his personal life—helping friends and family in need, assuming not-for-profit leadership, funding other small businesses or endeavors, signing on for too many philanthropic activities, or adopting an expensive lifestyle. The owner-manager may take some sizable distributions of profit, but if the business is growing, he is rarely able to take significant amounts of cash out of the business, so he may stretch himself too thin. Although personal financial obligations are usually not enough to create the need for a transaction, they can be significant enough for the owner-manager to be more swayed by the size of a cash offer than he should be.

Tom Johnston of the Doobie Brothers wittily wrote, "What were once vices are now habits." Once you become a supremely successful owner-manager, you are at risk of endangering your subjective well-being by unintentionally creating obligations for which you have no real passion. Your obligations frequently come from what seemed like a good idea—you thought you wanted (or "mis-wanted," as psychologists Daniel Gilbert and Timothy Wilson put it) that second or third house, a different spouse, a bigger boat, an Ivy League education for the kids—whatever—in the thought that attaining it would make you happy.

Gilbert says we are pathetic at forecasting what will make us happy. And because owner-managers frequently have reserves of mental and physical energy and the economic means to attain those things—they can get themselves into a position of life complexity very quickly without ever meaning to. Maybe for you it is the third home, the car collection, the LinkedIn relationships leading to networkers unproductively creating activity, not accomplishment—whatever it is, you have gone from the lightness of simplicity to the dizziness of complexity and the paradox of choice everywhere in your life.

The Moment Arrives

The owner-manager at last realizes—often with stunning force as well as some consternation—that he really needs to play a different role. He understands the enterprise has built a significant amount of value, that it may be time to realize some of that value, that he wants to determine the company's long-term future, and that he personally wants to be doing something different with his time.

3

Creating Enterprise Value

> Maximization of Opportunities is the meaningful, indeed
> precise definition of the entrepreneurial challenge. . . . The
> pertinent question is not how *to do things right*, but how
> to identify the *right things to do*, and to concentrate
> all your resources and efforts solely on them.
> —PETER F. DRUCKER

Do you ever ask yourself, "when is my 'someday'? when
should I plan to hand over the keys to another owner? When will
the value of the enterprise be so perfectly ripened that it is commercially irresistible? Does the success I have created have some kind of
shelf life such that I should try to sell out as soon as possible, before
it spoils? What am I worth?"

Sorry. *Wrong questions.*

The right question is: "As a manager, am I making decisions
that will advance the enterprise value for me as an owner, prepare
the organization for longevity beyond my time here, and allow the
opportunity for a capital gain someday?" *Someday.*

There is a spectrum of influencing factors, from industry dynamics to sheer luck, that affect the timing to such a degree as to make the date of "someday" imprecise, even unknowable. On the other hand, the arc of creating and increasing enterprise value *is* knowable, precise, and systematic. Executing on a plan to increase enterprise value involves work (and it can be hard work) that does more than add multiples to a closing price; it pumps strength and all kinds of good things into the enterprise—right now.

Passionately executing on a plan to increase enterprise value is where all good things come from. Do you want to increase your employees' success-sharing plan? *Execute on your plan to increase enterprise value.* Do you want more cash flow so you can borrow and expand or acquire new equipment? *Increase enterprise value.* Do you want to make distributions or pay dividends? *Increase enterprise value.* How about funding an employee stock ownership plan? *Increase enterprise value.* And, someday, do you want to attract the best possible strategic acquirers and private equity groups (PEGs) in the world to give you the opportunity to achieve a capital gain at an optimally high value? Then have the courage to take the actions necessary to increase enterprise value now. Think of it this way: increasing enterprise value now increases your company's sustainability for the long term, the really, really long term (the next hundred years) and for today, as well.

Here's what you need to do.

Speaking Truth = Leveraging Strength

Creating a highly successful enterprise, one that is recognizable and appealing to any potential new majority investor, cannot be accomplished in darkness. Although it may be counterintuitive to some owner-managers, and even seem reckless to others, it is essential to establish an environment of candor and clarity with your leadership team. Why? Building enterprise value can be hard work and demand tough calls, especially in the midst of a churning business with all of its insistent immediacy. Don't even consider working to build enterprise value if you aren't prepared to be intellectually and emotionally honest with yourself and your team about your professional and personal goals. The decisions made to increase enterprise value have implications across the organization—how you allocate human and financial resources, how you measure and assess your performance, and most important, how you shift the mindset from being stuck in the past or obsessed with the present to one focused sharply on the future.

The historical performance of your enterprise and all the stories and explanations about the "whys" around that performance cloud the air and affect your ability to shift the focus to the future. Many management teams (and even owners) feel threatened and become defensive when historical performance is at the center of the discussion. They have become attached to the lore of their success, and their natural tendency is to argue against any view of it that might diminish its luster. That's human and understandable, *and* it has no place in the forward-looking efforts of building enterprise value.

Radical Transparency

The antidote, in our experience, is transparency, what I call "radical transparency." Everyone on the strategic team (including your advisors) must be willing and able to engage and speak openly with each other as equals in the challenge of building enterprise value. There's no place for hierarchy, hidden alliances, or off-line discussions when the real decisions are being made. Everyone on your strategic team should have access to all information without exception. Radical? Maybe. But these group members are privileged to be included in such a candid discussion about the company's future precisely *because* they are senior management members who bear the enormous responsibility for directing and implementing the work of increasing enterprise value. It's their shared responsibility, and they alone bear it.

Your strategic team is swimming in confidential information—they must be. They must also understand that it would be manifestly unfair—no, it would be reckless—for them to share any of this confidential information with people outside the strategy team. This kind of sharing is irresponsible, because it is always without context and always spreads anxiety. It's manifestly unfair for the senior team to inject uncertainty into the lives of non–senior management employees. Just at the moment when the business needs everyone performing at his or her best, rumors bring out the worst. That's damaging to even the most enlightened efforts elsewhere in the company to cultivate and increase enterprise value. In my experience, the two guidelines that simply can't be violated are these: within the room there is absolute transparency; out of the room there is absolute confidentiality. Let's get to work.

When a Bigelow Team begins to work with an owner-managed business on creating enterprise value, we often start the conversation offsite. The session includes the owner-manager and a half dozen (or fewer) senior members of the management team. Here's a powerful way for the owner-manager to open the session: "Let's stipulate right now that absolutely every decision we made in the past was a good one. They were each made for excellent reasons based upon the information available at that time. We aren't here to critique the past. We are here to talk about the changes we should consider now to become the organization we need to be in the future."

The partnering process between company and advisor can only succeed through a combination of this kind of radical transparency coupled with absolute confidentially. Just as it was difficult for Ann Farrell, mentioned in Chapter 2, to share performance data with her second-tier management team, it can be even more difficult for the owner-manager to release information to people who are essentially strangers. But the best partnerships are based on the deepest possible knowledge of one another.

The Enterprise Value Equation

Coming out of these sessions, you and your team should have a clear understanding of the simplified enterprise value equation: enterprise value = (EBITDA × multiple). The value is always reduced to this basic calculation. EBITDA (pronounced "E-bidda")—earnings before interest, taxes, depreciation, and amortization—is multiplied by a number that is largely related to the attractiveness of your industry and modified by specific qualitative and quantitative factors of your own organization.

There are lots of components that go into EBITDA that are known. (See Figure 3.1.) And there are a million and one things that

FIGURE 3.1 How Should Stockholders Think about Valuation?
M&A Valuation Shorthand: EBITDA Multiples

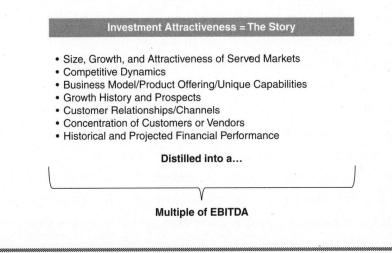

Investment Attractiveness = The Story

- Size, Growth, and Attractiveness of Served Markets
- Competitive Dynamics
- Business Model/Product Offering/Unique Capabilities
- Growth History and Prospects
- Customer Relationships/Channels
- Concentration of Customers or Vendors
- Historical and Projected Financial Performance

Distilled into a...

Multiple of EBITDA

affect the multiple, but the result of that application of art and science always gets distilled down to this formula.

So it all begins with EBITDA. The best way to know—really *know*—your EBITDA is with the accuracy of audited financial statements over a number of years. It's what potential investors are likely to insist on: several years of audited financial statements—not compiled, not reviewed, but audited—by a reputable certified public accounting firm. This kind of discipline is what building enterprise value looks like.

If you have created an advisory board of external, nonmanagement, nonfamily observers, board members can be engaged in the process. Sometimes their role is formally recognized and integrated into the organization; sometimes the board is informally assembled to address specific challenges. What the best advisory boards share is a clear mandate to offer objective counsel and practiced expertise. The high-functioning advisory boards I have seen are dynamic and generative forums; they act as knowledge resources and feedback loops for the owner-manager. It's like a "master class in my own business," as one owner-manager put it. What he also discovered was that his advisory board provided a critical training forum where he could get better at presenting his business to groups of potential investors. The advisory board members can ask questions that a potential owner might ask from the position of someone who is not an owner or intending to be.

David Cooperrider, an expert in organizational behavior, suggests that query and change are simultaneous. A query does not necessarily require an answer to bring about change; usually simply focusing on the right questions can bring about needed positive organizational changes. One of the less understood benefits of building enterprise value is also one of its most powerful: building upside for the next majority investor. After all, your good work at the exit is their momentum at the entrance, and momentum earns a premium.

Clients have repeatedly told me how the following exercise of asking four key questions has had a positive impact on them, their team, and their business model, even if they chose not to go immediately to a wealth creation transaction.

All kinds of good things happen when turf battles and politics are banished and you examine your organization through the eyes of an outside investor. In my experience, buyers are going to ask, in essence, four questions. They are not the kinds of questions managers ask; they are the kinds of questions owners ask. Owners ask them and then *act* upon them as they steer the enterprise forward.

The Four Most Important Questions for You (and all Investors)

The balance of this chapter is devoted to asking—and guiding you as you answer—the four most important questions that affect enterprise value and that someday, potential majority investors are going to seek to answer (see Figure 3.2). Your answers are the measure of

FIGURE 3.2   Key Long-Term Drivers of Enterprise Value

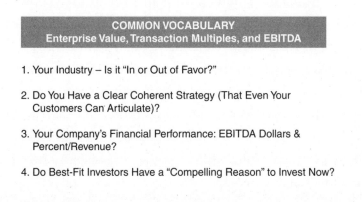

COMMON VOCABULARY
Enterprise Value, Transaction Multiples, and EBITDA

1. Your Industry – Is it "In or Out of Favor?"

2. Do You Have a Clear Coherent Strategy (That Even Your Customers Can Articulate)?

3. Your Company's Financial Performance: EBITDA Dollars & Percent/Revenue?

4. Do Best-Fit Investors Have a "Compelling Reason" to Invest Now?

the enterprise value you've created and are creating. Resist the temptation to view these questions as a final exam. Instead, think of them as periodic inspections of your own mindset, opportunities to recalibrate your actions and direct the organization's forward progress toward a "someday" destination.

1. Industry In or Out of Favor with Institutional Investors

Does the size, growth rate, and attractiveness of your industry allow for a capital gain someday? This is the first question because it's the most important one . . . and the one most misunderstood. People at my company have seen many well-managed businesses with impressive market shares fail to create a capital gain event that reflected an owner-manager's hard work and smart decisions. It can be particularly heartbreaking to observe, especially when many owner-managers did the right things to increase enterprise value but their industry was temporarily out of favor with institutional investors. Maybe the overall market they inhabited was shrinking, or perhaps customer consolidation had reduced opportunities and lowered margins. As counterintuitive as it sounds, sometimes dominating a small market can actually reduce appeal by narrowing the perceived potential for growth.

To determine if a capital gain is in your future, knowledge—objective and comprehensive—is vital. The first thing to know is the true size of the addressable market and how quickly it's growing. Your addressable market is always smaller than the entire global market; *addressable* means what it says: with a reasonable effort and investment, what could your business attain as its share of market? Slow-growth or shrinking markets may be fine places to live for a while, maybe even a long while, but the next majority investor isn't looking for "fine."

If the addressable market is growing, the next question is "why?" What are the drivers of the underlying growth in demand? The answers to those questions can be stubbornly opaque, especially to owner-managers looking from the inside out. Owner-managers are notoriously poor evaluators of their own industries; it's not that they lack the analytical tools, but that their views of the industry have narrowed over time. The demands of leading a business day to day tend to accentuate the inner hedgehog that knows one thing very well. What's needed to accurately answer broader questions on industry size and growth is the fox who knows many things.

The size of the addressable market is the first issue related to your industry; the next two concern your share of market and the competitive environment. Some of the questions you should be able to answer: *Where does my company lead? Where do we follow? Who (and where) is the price leader? Who discounts their price? Who and what are driving prices higher or lower? Who has the lowest overall costs? Who has the lowest cost per unit (so that at a given market price they make the highest profit)?*

There is some overlap with these questions and those that define the overall market, such as the question of how well the industry as a whole delivers value to its customer base. Decoding the industry value chain and knowing your role within it is vital to building enterprise value toward the eventual capital gain.

Then we come to the competition. It's essential to see deeply into how your competitors operate. *What are they doing that's similar to what you do? What are they doing differently?* Advisors can help with this. For example, in my company, we as outsiders bring an objective point of view to the decisions your competition is making. We will look at how they allocate resources compared to how your enterprise allocates and examine in detail their strategic intent. It's easier for us to engage your competitors directly than it is for you to do so.

And even if your competitors won't talk to us, it's not hard to gather information about them. They can be studied at industry events and trade shows.

Your advisors on the floor can ask a lot of questions—about your competition and about your business, and the answers rarely fail to enlighten. In certain cases advisors will partner with a world-class third-party strategy consulting firm to research the world addressable market, growth rates, competitive mapping, and opportunity.

The work of answering this first question that investors will eventually ask invariably creates some tension. The inside view is almost always different than the outside view. The hedgehog and the fox don't immediately appreciate the other's way of seeing the world, but there's a need for both when enterprise value is being built. What works in these engagements is taking a new view of a familiar space.

Science Specialties

That's exactly how it happened with Science Specialties, a business based in the western United States. Its owners described the company as "a manufacturer of science lab countertops used in schools." (Remember those black indestructible laboratory countertops you leaned your elbows on as you suffered through high school chemistry?) Science Specialties was into its third decade, generating about $50 million in revenue with above-average profitability. At Bigelow, as our understanding of their industry grew, we saw how their concentration on schools had not only sharpened their focus but also limited their view. Science Specialties' industry, as the company defined it, was a $100 million to $125 million business and growing slowly. After the first stages of our work, which included looking closely inside and outside the company, we saw it differently. Science Specialties wasn't just in the school science lab business; it was really a small player in the larger "solid surface manufacturing" business. And in that business, there certainly are important customers in schools, but they can also be found in hospitals and life science labs, in manufacturers that need industrial-strength surfaces, even in restaurants and other institutions that require tough table surfaces. Now *that* industry as defined is a billion-dollar industry and growing fast, right alongside healthcare and life science. When we advisors shared our views with the management team they quickly (to their credit) grasped what we were talking about: "Yes, yes . . . I guess that's right. We've actually been thinking we ought to spend some time brainstorming about that idea and talking about the larger market. But honestly, we've been so busy driving the day-to-day business we simply haven't had the time to look at the forest instead of the trees."

Compare a business with a 50 percent share of market in a flat demand environment to a business with a small but unique and defensible niche of a fast-growing industry. Which would you invest in first? The difference is not trivial. Warren Buffett is said to have remarked, "When it comes to strategy, what matters most is what business boat you are in, not how hard you row." How you define your business model—your "business boat"—has implications across every aspect of the strategy: resource allocation, leadership and staffing, manufacturing technology, and marketing investments.

This accurately captures my view on how important your industry is to driving your enterprise value. Nothing is more important to enterprise value than the industry you inhabit. Nothing. To be clear, it's good to row hard, to strive and challenge your managers. Managing well is good. And good management is better than bad management. But when good management meets bad industry, the out-of-favor industry's depressing effect on enterprise value *overcomes good management every time*—every single time.

When industries go into favor with institutional investors, valuations expressed as multiples of EBITDA go up. When industries are out of favor with institutional investors, multiples decline. Do a little simple arithmetic here. Multiply your current EBITDA by a favorable industry multiple, say 8 times EBITDA. So if your EBITDA is $10 million when your industry is in favor, the enterprise value is $80 million, right? Now multiply your same current EBITDA ($10 million) times an unfavorable industry multiple, say 5. When the industry goes out of favor, the enterprise value is $50 million. Ouch. Now let's compute: what would your EBITDA dollars have to grow to in order to achieve the $80 million enterprise value at the lower out-of-favor industry multiple? The answer is $16 million. Just how many years do you think it would take you to grow your EBITDA from $10 to $16 million? Do you appreciate the difficulty, how challenging it is, to grow EBITDA by 60 percent from $10 million to $16 million? Many—most—businesses never get there. That's what I mean by saying that nothing is more impactful on enterprise value than the industry you are in, and whether or not it is in or out of favor now.

So determining if your industry is in or out of favor involves more than lining up rows in a spreadsheet and crunching them into something digestible. It's also about asking open-ended questions and experimenting with a point of view. For owner-managers, this can be both disorienting and exhilarating. That said, it's not for every business.

Some good businesses simply don't have an opportunity for a capital gain. For example, law firms do not; the assets leave in the elevator, and there's no replicable methodology that can be leveraged, improved, or delivered "one to many." Many talent-rich professional service firms are in a similar situation. It's not inherently bad, it just is. Their business models are essentially one-to-one and dependent upon the skill and craft of individual practitioners.

Other businesses have allowed themselves to align with a few high-volume customers—sometimes just one. As we saw with Jeff and Victory Windows, inside that concentrated big-box customer there's risk for the owner-manager and poison for most investors. When there is a massive scale difference, large concentrated customers can dictate terms. Financial investors will be unable to attract and secure senior debt financing (and so will you), since lenders understand the capricious nature of these relationships.

If you are in an industry that doesn't afford a capital gain, or if you have gotten yourself into a customer concentration situation that inhibits it, the best course may be to maximize the cash flow and distribute it to shareholders each year. For owner-managers in this type of industry, enterprise value is something that is captured *as it's created*. The end number may fall far short of a true capital gain, but it's better to understand this early in the life cycle and set stakeholder expectations accordingly.

2. Do You Have a Simple, Clear, and Coherent Strategy?

Strategy can be a muddy place for many owner-managers. Successful customer segmenting, specialty markets, or good execution can easily be mistaken for an overall company strategy. And it's fair to ask why your strategy matters when you might not even be leading the execution under the next majority owner. However, as mentioned earlier, that next investor is acquiring *everything* you've done right to build enterprise value (that includes a sound strategy to grow the business) and is actually growing the business right now.

The best strategies are the simplest. For example, every decision made by Southwest Airlines must pass through its strategy to be the low-cost leader in air travel. It's how the company evaluates everything. There's no ambiguity and no MBA required. Your own strategy should be equally clear and visible to everyone in the value chain. If it is that simple, then your employees, your advisors, and *even your customers* should be able to say it in a single sentence.

When building enterprise value, clear and coherent strategies are internal guidelines on how to allocate the finite resources available to you . . . human expressions like energy, passion, and urgency, as well as cash and technology. The bookshelf is rich with titles that take you deep into the bowels of business strategy. Bruce Hendersen, Michael Porter, David Maister, Clay Christensen, and others have written intelligently and thoughtfully about strategy. But building enterprise value, at least in the stages we're focused on here, has less to do with theoretical strategy development and more to do with its practical application.

Answering the second question actually involves asking a barrage of others. Here is a preliminary list:

- What is your purpose?
- What is your competitive strategy within your industry?
- Construct a preliminary strategy hypothesis.
- Specifically, what is your business model?
- What is your value proposition to customers? What are your unique capabilities so you deliver such great value to your customers that they allow you to price for an exceptional profit?
- What kinds of customers are you trying to attract?
- Do you have exceptional customer relationships and/or a unique marketing and selling channel to them?
- What kinds of customers are you absolutely willing to repel and systematically discard?
- Do you have really persuasive evidence of what you consider to be special customer relationships such as metrics on the average customer longevity, repeat order rate, growth in revenues by customer, and gross margin improvements by customer?

- Do you have superior financial performance that validates your value proposition to customers?
- Are you reinvesting into the business at the optimal rate?
- Do you have channel clarity, with a proprietary or at least highly disciplined way you go to market?

The last question is timely because there is a proliferation of channel confusion today. Blame it on the Internet and the murkiness between wholesale and retail. Recently, people at my company have witnessed many consumer product companies that began in wholesale and then added a retail presence to build brand awareness. First they exist on wholesale customers, then they print an expensive catalog, and next they add an expensive website. And they frequently add expensive retail stores (which may compete with the original wholesale customers). When we ask owner-managers at these companies what business they are in, or what are the most important or successful channels for them, they are often unsure of or unclear about the answer. For these owner-managers, financial results are always below average, which is understandable, as they are dividing finite resources among multiple channels with uncertain effectiveness. There's nothing simple about that strategy.

Diversification within a Business Destroys Enterprise Value

A deeply treasured narrative fallacy with untested entrepreneur business owners is that diversification within one's own business makes it attractive to acquirers. At first blush, that seems sensible, right? *If I sell big pieces of expensive equipment to Market A, and small pieces of unrelated equipment to Market B, then I am protected because chances are when Market A is up, Market B will be down, and vice versa.* Untrue. In fact, nothing could be *more* wrong in building enterprise value. Diversification *within* a business *always* decreases

91

enterprise value. Sustained enterprise value is created by concentrating on one business. Investors want to invest in specific "pure-play" businesses in niche markets. They may want to have a diversified portfolio of businesses, but if they do, they want a portfolio of multiple businesses—each one a pure play in its own market. Investors are acquiring the future potential of your business, not its past. So develop supportable and defensible growth strategies and execute them boldly. Your success in a focused and growing pure-play niche business will attract the right acquirer someday. Need more proof? Check the price/earnings multiple of almost any diversified company compared to the P/E multiple of a pure-play niche player.

3. Does Your Superior Financial Performance Validate Your Strategy?

Specifically, how profitable is your profit? The second most important driver of enterprise value (after the industry you are in) is your EBITDA percentage *measured as a percentage of sales* and whether or not it is superior to your industry.

An exceptional profit (measured in actual EBITDA dollars but, more importantly, as a percentage of revenues) compared to your industry tells objective outsiders whether your customers genuinely value what you are providing to them, and are willing to pay for it. *That's* the point of profit in the eyes of investors. They are not interested in profit for profit's sake, nor is any other sensible objective outsider. Advisors and investors view profit as the essential blood of the organization through which the oxygen of cash flows. Cash flow is essential working capital: investments in growth, the *profit* in *profit sharing*.

Advisors and investors look at the financial performance metrics that the biggest entrants in your industry use, and then they decide whether to use or modify them as they evaluate your performance.

This doesn't mean you run the business on other people's metrics; it just means you think about them and take them into account before and after the fact. It's rarely easy to shift your team's attention, focus, and reporting away from historical earnings and toward *projected* EBITDA, but the fact is your next majority investor simply is not focusing much on historical earnings except as a context for the validity of your future growth plan.

Historical internal financial statements give management teams the latitude to use different accounting methods that deliver different earnings reports. Beyond that, earnings don't reflect working capital requirements such as the need for higher receivables or more inventory. Nor do they reflect the need for larger capital expenditures. Establishing the cost of inventory and the rate of depreciation are management choices that can be defended under a dizzying variety of interpretations. What can look like earnings are really justifications, which gets to a deeper and more troubling truth: in some organizations there are cultural impediments to high profits.

Eastland Farms

Michael Jones established Eastland Farms, a fresh food distributor that had earned a solid reputation as a quality source of good-tasting products. Annual sales grew to $110 million, but the company was always running scared. As Mike warned his children who worked in the business, "If you want to get rich, don't come into the family business." He did his best to keep them away too, even the ones who were actually in the business. Mike isolated himself. He scoffed at the "waste of time" of trade associations or CEO peer groups, and he operated in constant fear of the national food companies whose sheer size translated into purchasing advantages. He resented the massive leverage the most important supermarket chain customers wielded.

When Mike died, there were eight family members in the business, and his son Jack reluctantly took the reins of an organization with an energy-draining culture and an anemic EBITDA. Eastland's EBITDA was stuck in the single digits, while best performers in the industry had high-double-digit EBITDA/net revenue. Not only was the company *not* making a high profit computed as a percentage of sales, it viewed any discussion of profit improvement with a degree of suspicion. Higher profit might mean higher prices, right? And after all, an articulated desire for high profits would translate into evidence of the family's obvious "greed," wouldn't it? Despite the food distributor's strong reputation, Jack and the rest of the family remained fearful that the loss of any one customer and its accompanying unit volume would put Eastland immediately into a loss position. They had good reasons to be tentative; the company's below-average profitability and cash flow over the years had inhibited its ability to reinvest in the business technology, and the lack of information limited the ability to make tough but necessary decisions about which customers to keep and which ones to fire. Jack and the rest of the family came to my company to discuss and explore attracting a new owner. These were difficult conversations for all the reasons you see here, and more. But there were also "aha moments" around the importance of profits and the cultural drag that had diminished them. Eastland is a work in progress. The company is changing; it is focused on profitability as confirmation of value to the customer; and its enterprise value is growing. Someday the next majority investor should appreciate the company's efforts to connect the value delivered to profits earned.

Surprised to see cultural language when the question is financial performance? The connection is closer than you might think.

When your company is delivering high value to the customer, then you've earned the right to a high profit computed as a percentage of sales. For purely objective outside observers of your business, a high EBITDA as a percentage of sales, more than almost any other metric, signals that customers value your products and services. Those customer perceptions are a powerful component in the building of enterprise value, but they aren't the only perceptions that matter. Investors also look for a deeply held confidence by your management team that you *deserve* all the profits you generate because you perform at the highest levels. This high-performance, high-profit culture is a powerful contributor to building enterprise value. Without it, in my experience, it is unlikely a company will get its entire team fully on board. To take a company that accepts poor or even average performance and turn it into a superior-performing company almost always takes a significant emotional event: a change of ownership, not merely a change of management. This brings us to the fourth question.

4. Attraction: Can We Find the Best-Fit Investor Who Has a Compelling Reason to Invest Now?

Here's a qualifying statement if there ever was one: the best-fit investors already have it in their mind (and even in their business plan) to be in your business. Ideally, they have been attracted to your industry because of its inherent characteristics, and they are already thinking about (or executing on) a plan to enter the industry de novo or by acquisition. For M&A advisors like Bigelow, these are satisfying dialogues to enter into with potential investors because advisors can move quickly to understand their growth strategies and determine if learning about your company is an opportunity for them. Sometimes however, the challenge is moving toward the best-fit investor by changing the kind of business you're in. That's what Eastern Machine Company (EMCo) did.

Increase Enterprise Value = Increase Business Longevity

Following the strategies to optimize enterprise value as the business matures results in generation of alternatives for a capital gain someday. Figure 3.3 summarizes our discussion here. More importantly, it creates a business that has sustainability and longevity beyond you, the personal owner of it. In the next chapter, we explore the ambiguities of an opaque and mysterious place: the private company transaction market.

FIGURE 3.3   Shareholder Value Benchmark

Industry Dynamics	Corporate Strategy	Operational Efficiency	Financial Performance
• Competitive Landscape • Sustainable Levels of Profitability • Market Size & Growth • Fragmentation or Concentration • Capital Requirements • Drivers of Value	• Differentiation • Mission & Vision • Regimented Methodologies • Management Capability/Depth • Proprietary Process or Brand	• Productivity • Asset Turnover • Operating Leverage • Measureable Outcomes • Revenue per Employee • Balance Sheet Management	• Revenue & Earnings Growth • Gross & Operating Margins • Reinvestment History • Asset Base/Usage • Sustainability • ROI

Identify Global Value Drivers | **Benchmark Relevant Business Metrics**

Critical Assessment

Action Steps to Build Shareholder Value

4

Seller Beware: The Private Transaction Market

> As they say in poker, if you've been in the game thirty minutes
> and you don't know who the patsy is, *you're the patsy.*
>
> —WARREN BUFFETT

THE PRIVATE COMPANY TRANSACTION MARKET IS NOT QUITE THE Wild Wild West, but it's pretty close. The market itself has no stock exchange, physical or electronic. There are no set hours when transactions must, or do, take place. Private companies themselves have no public financial reporting requirements. There is no financial transparency in this environment—the Sarbanes-Oxley and Dodd-Frank Acts do not apply. There is no equivalent of the Standard & Poor's 500 average (S&P 500) or the Dow Jones Industrial Average (DJIA) to give you an aggregate measure of how the market is priced. There are no price/earnings ratios and no published research. No betas are calculated here.

The skills needed to succeed in the private company transaction market are quite different from those prized in the public markets.

What matters with this market are hard-earned experience, skill in dealing with asymmetrical information, and highly motivated, savvy, and often difficult people. What matters less are academic credentials or whether you've put in five-plus years as an analyst with a full-service financial firm (insert logo of your choice here). No, it's not quite the Wild Wild West, but it is a place to buckle up and pay close attention to the fact that you are operating at the intersection of psychology and finance.

I'm about to generalize, not because I intend to blunt a nuanced dialogue, but because the subject at hand, the private transaction market, requires aggregating advisors' experience and generalizing in order to learn from it. First, some definitions. The private transaction market is populated by three kinds of investors: the strategic investor (strategic), the private equity group (PEG), and the private equity platform (platform). There is also an interesting subcategory of the PEG, the family office, which we'll consider in a moment. The first two major types of investor—strategics and PEGs—are utterly different species, one from the other, while the third is a hybrid, combining some of the characteristics of the other two. Each has a "personality" that, generally speaking, is knowable. The question for you, the owner-manager, is which kind of investor can you influence or even proactively choose to become the best next majority owner of your business? (See Figure 4.1.) Do different types of capital have different investor personalities? Does it matter for the legacy of your company? And, how do you know the good people from the bad people?

Strategic Investors: The New General Manager

Strategic investors may bring some synergistic benefit to your business. They may already be in your industry, be in one of the industries adjacent to it, or just have it in their business plan to enter it. Strategic

FIGURE 4.1 What Kind of Investor Makes Sense? Comparison of Strategic Acquirer and Financial Investor Types

Each type of capital has a different "personality." They are seeking different goals, thus they frequently provide significantly different alternatives.

	STRATEGIC INVESTOR	PRIVATE EQUITY PLATFORM INVESTOR	PRIVATE EQUITY INVESTOR
LIQUIDITY	100%	←	51%–80% initially
VALUATION	Synergistic benefits may create premium valuation	→	Based on potential IRR of growth business plan
FUTURE UPSIDE	Typically limited	←	Two bites of the apple may provide most aggregate value
GOVERNANCE	Report to acquirer's management	→	Board of directors, with investor representatives
OPERATIONAL CHANGE	Brings preexisting model	→	Mostly financial/reporting in nature
CULTURE	Assimilate to parent's	→	Augmented by new constituencies
CAPITALIZATION	Potentially stronger balance sheet and flexibility	→	Leveraged stand-alone balance sheet
STRATEGY	Must fit previously identified strategic direction of acquirer	→	Double sales and EBITDA
EMPLOYEES/ MANAGEMENT	May broaden (or shorten) employees' career path	←	Equity upside for key employees

investors may be your competitors, suppliers, or even your customers. My experience is that more often than not you've never heard of them or are not familiar with them because they aren't directly connected to your industry but work alongside it—for example, selling different products to the same customers or addressable market.

The best strategics already have it in their business plan to be in the business you are in. So when they are approached by an advisory firm like mine, on behalf of a firm like yours, the opportunity the advisors are introducing to them is already on their strategic "list of things to do." Frequently these companies are large ones and often publicly owned, and often they have a strategy for and a track record of growing by acquisition.

Strategic investors almost always want to acquire 100 percent of your business, largely for accounting and tax reasons. That can mean they want to purchase everything and everyone associated with your company, in certain cases including you. When a strategic investor wants to hire you as part of its investment, it can be a jarring experience for you, a self-directed, lifelong owner-manager. You may never have worked for anybody else in your entire life. Now suddenly you are reporting to a boss, and that person, in a strategic investor firm, tends to be a bureaucratic manager who's there to run a process . . . *his* process. But wait! What about all that conversation you had with the strategic investor during the acquisition process when it asked about your company's culture and your management style and all of that? Yes, it was sincere in its interest, but not because it wanted to preserve or emulate the culture you had in place. It was gathering important information that would help the company evaluate the challenges of absorbing your culture into *its* culture.

Don't despair. There is plenty of good news. Strategics usually have intelligence about their own markets and the markets they have targeted to enter. They usually have a plan and a strategy to achieve it. They are (or should be) well financed, and the acquisition of your firm shouldn't stress them financially. (If it would, the strategic is not a good candidate.) They didn't get to their successful position without intelligence and above-average execution skills. And your employees will get something that was almost certainly limited before the strategic appeared on the scene: upward career mobility. After all, you had the top job, and the career path for everyone else was probably a lot shorter, with fewer options, than the multiple winding paths available in a large, multisite strategic. There are other reasons to like strategic investors, and we'll get to those soon.

Lundberg Corporation: A Case for the Strategic Investor

In what circumstances might a strategic acquirer be the best next majority owner of your business?

That was essentially the question on the table at the first meeting my partners and I had with the three passive majority owners of the Lundberg Corporation: "What kind of acquirer would be the best one for the long-term sustainability and success for the stakeholders of the company?" Lundberg is in the business of making seals for automotive and defense aerospace applications—principally engine systems. The company, which is over a hundred years old, started making its seals out of leather, and gradually it progressed to early types of rubber, then plastic, and finally specialty elastomeric compounds. It buys the raw materials from vendors, who mix them to Lundberg's spec, and then compression-molds them into small mission-critical parts of extremely precise dimensions.

Let's first consider what a private equity group might offer. A PEG acquisition could certainly result in a good outcome for the Lundberg management team because they would retain some ownership, but the deal would also probably leverage the company's own balance sheet by senior debt borrowings. [This would juice up the PEG's return on investment, measured as its internal rate of return (IRR).] Lundberg had survived the 2008–2009 automotive recession, during which units produced in North America dropped from an annual run rate of 17 million to 7 million. It had reduced its number of plants from three to one, laid off hundreds of workers, and emerged with a company that had lower overhead, was more productive, and had a more competitive product offering. The management team was going to be skeptical of any plans that the PEG's "financial engineers" might have for layering the company with debt that was unrelated to making the business more viable for the long term. They had too much skin in the game not to care—and to care deeply.

Now, it may sound surprising that a supplier to the automotive and aerospace industries would be an attractive candidate for acquisition by any kind of investor. Isn't the automotive industry working to reduce, not increase, the number of vendors it works with? And isn't that also true of the maturing defense aerospace industry? Aren't both industries experiencing slow growth?

The answers are yes. And, in a low-growth-rate industry like automotive, when manufacturing productivity increases, the result can often be overcapacity. Ideally, the new majority owner would understand all this and bring something to the table—in addition to capital, of course—that would enable Lundberg to be one of the survivors in the industry. Better yet, the investor would help Lundberg become a standout: a well-capitalized innovator, with special expertise in a relevant discipline such as elastomeric material science, and even deeper know-how of manufacturing, such that it could churn out a billion parts per year at critically high tolerances and low failure rates.

After lengthy discussions with several major European and North American strategics and some of the best PEGs in the world, Lundberg's owners decided to negotiate exclusively with a strategic, Shen Yang Manufacturing, an entrepreneur-led company based in mainland China. Shen Yang had long been a significant supplier to Asian automotive manufacturers. More recently, through a plant it had acquired in Detroit, it was becoming an important source for North American manufacturers as well. Interestingly enough, many of the European and American strategics I spoke with had a low opinion of their own business because of the difficulties of the automotive industry. Not Shen Yang. Not only did the folks at Shen Yang understand the drivers of competition, they welcomed the idea that they could go even deeper into the automotive industry in North America through the acquisition of Lundberg. The company was 100 percent engaged in the manufacture of components used in seal applications, including some adjacent to (but not competitive with) Lundberg.

As is customarily the case with strategics, the due diligence investigation of Lundberg proceeded a lot more easily and faster than it would have with a PEG. Where a PEG might require a third-party market study or endless customer calls and interviewing, a strategic like Shen Yang didn't need a third-party market study—after all, it was already heavily in the market. It didn't need to speak with customers, because it had the same customers as Lundberg. If the Shen Yang people felt they had needed to do a sanity check with customers at all, it would have been in a friendly, reasonably casual way.

We at Bigelow worked hard to establish a relationship of mutual trust, largely by being radically transparent, and that helped us get to a preliminary offer very quickly. First, we discussed Lundberg's desired transaction structure (all cash) and Shen Yang's interest in having some payments contingent on Lundberg's performance. Ultimately we were able to convince Shen Yang that it's not a good idea to include contingent payments to passive owners in the deal. It keeps the owners interested in the company longer, while Shen Yang wanted to make changes reasonably quickly and according to its own business plan (which our management agreed with).

From that point, the negotiation was relatively straightforward and not complex. We at Bigelow established some talking points around valuation (driven by the fair market multiples of similar companies), and Shen Yang was able to respond quickly, through its North American attorneys, with a letter of intent. Because we had established a high level of credibility and trust with people at Shen Yang, they were willing to be coached on "what is market" (price, terms, and conditions) even though we, as advisors, technically represented "the other side."

Although the negotiation was straightforward, the parties faced a number of cultural and regulatory hurdles, but because we both had the incentive to get the transaction closed by year's end, we were able to work cooperatively to get over them. There was the usual last-minute attempt to retrade on price and rework a few of the terms (this is not unusual in a negotiation with a strategic), but when all of these were solidly rebuffed, Shen Yang did not push them further and moved on to closing. Lundberg's management team is now a key part of Shen Yang's North American organization and is eagerly looking forward to advancing the company as a global supplier to automotive and aerospace seal applications.

Private Equity Groups: Partners in Profit

Private equity groups (PEGs) have simple needs: they love to invest in well-run companies with high growth potential, and they need *you* to help them make it happen for them. A PEG is in it for the money, some of which is yours. Unlike the strategics, which always want to own 100 percent of your business, PEGs *always* want to own *less* than 100 percent, and they always want to share ownership with you as a shareholder, current management, or both. The sellers, or their management team, typically have "skin in the game" going forward in the range of 10 to 20 percent total ownership of the recapitalized company's equity. They figure that if you are, and if you act in the best interest of your 20 percent ownership, then their 80 percent ownership will be just fine.

PEGs aren't operators, and they aren't historians either. They only care about how your business has performed in previous years as a context for the future. PEGs measure performance in EBITDA and, generally speaking, they look to double your current EBITDA over the next five years, ideally paying down the debt they borrowed while doing so. After that period of time, they want to exit the investment with the enterprise value at two to three times what it was when they first invested.

Unlike strategics, then, PEGs are not in the effort for the long haul. They may say they intend to hold companies for 7 to 10 years, but my experience strongly suggests the average is closer to 3 to 5 years. In fact, their very structure focuses them on their next exit.

Why is this? *Because it's not their money.* They have to give it back. PEGs attract outside investors just as any other fund manager does when making a pitch to the street. And PEGs have been pitching hard in recent years. They have raised hundreds of billions of dollars that are still to be invested, which, with leverage, gives them investment capacity of over $1 trillion looking for a place to work. PEGs can't sit there counting it. They are incentivized personally and professionally to invest it.

These investment pools are in the form of limited partnerships, and they have a finite life, usually 10 years. Read a PEG limited partnership document some time. Typically, the PEG is restricted and can only invest a certain percentage of its fund (say, 10 percent) in any one company. That makes perfect sense for the LP investor, doesn't it? If the PEG has a $250 million fund, and it can borrow that same amount, it can spend $500 million. It then makes 10 investments, paying $50 million for each one of them.

Then PEG people go to work with the owner-manager and her or his management team, to increase enterprise value. And the effort succeeds. Let's say the enterprise value of a company the PEG acquired grows from $50 million to $100 million over five years. Now the PEG's fund has a disproportionate amount of its value in one ($100 million) investment. No wonder that, as the enterprise value of the company grew, the PEG leadership became increasingly hesitant about new capital investment and probably reined in the management team for the last couple of years. According to the deal with the PEG's limited partners, it is incentivized to lock the gain by exiting. Then, in order for other PEGs to be attracted to the company, which now has an enterprise value of $100 million, the company is recapitalized by a new PEG with a $500 million fund in order to adhere to the investment ratios. Its ambition will be to double the $100 million enterprise value to $200 million, reigniting the management team's aggressive growth plan, and accelerating the entrepreneurial machine back to its optimal speed.

Unlike owner-managers who are principals, PEGs are agents for the limited partners who provide nearly all the capital to their funds. And the most desirable way for them to repay their limited partners (and, beyond repayment, *reward* them with a nice return) is to sell the business and get liquid. And that's where you and your shareholders and management team stand to earn a reward of your own.

Remember, the PEG already paid you 80 to 90 percent of the enterprise value, but you and/or your team still own 10 to 20 percent of the business. When the PEG exits and hands off to a new majority investor, your 10 to 20 percent is now calculated at its (presumably higher) valuation. This is what some finance wonks call "two bites of the apple." You have "one bite" where you get paid for 80 percent of your ownership. You get the "second bite" when you and the PEG sell the ownership and you have 20 percent. We've seen many successful teams stay in place as two or even three PEG investor groups acquire and then resell the business, taking a stake and then taking another bite with each exit. Good for them. These are almost always individuals who wouldn't have any other way to access those outsized capital gains, and it results in significant wealth creation for them, their families, and their communities.

PEGs—especially the largest and the most leveraged of them—have taken a few hits in recent media reports. Their voracious appetite for growth and earnings has led them to make some bad calls on good businesses; perhaps they've earned the criticism. But in my experience in the aggregate, my company's clients have done well with PEGs; the enterprise value of each of their businesses has grown significantly after the first transaction. The key is knowing who these groups are serving and having insight to their EBITDA-driven view of the world. If you can demonstrate the right potential for growth, they *want* to fund it. Like other investors, every private equity group has an identifiable personality, and that personality will have an impact on you, if it becomes your partner. There are good people out there and some not so good people. It's up to reputable M&A advisory firms like ours to help you navigate your way through this channel. It's worth underlining: from my point of view what PEGs represent is capital, which is a fungible commodity—you can rent it at basically the same rate from anyone. What your company represents is the truly scarce and valuable thing: a successful, privately owned niche business.

TechEdge: A Private Equity Group Recapitalization

Let's go into more detail of how a PEG recapitalization deal goes, by telling the story of TechEdge, a firm that designs and manufactures components for computer server racks, including structural components and integrated cooling devices (since the servers in the racks are a source of great heat).

TechEdge had been acquired from the founder by a family who then owned the company for 20 years. As the computer hardware industry matured, the number of potential customers dwindled and the concentration increased (as did the risk inherent in too much customer concentration). A husband-and-wife team, Pat and Lisa Snell, ran the business. Pat was technical and operations oriented, and Lisa was skilled in finance and administration. Both had MBAs, one from Harvard and one from MIT. Together they possessed much of the functional ability needed for executive leadership, but running the business together had taken a toll on their family life. They found it difficult to have dinner or enjoy a few days of vacation without the family business being the number-one topic of conversation.

But Pat and Lisa were unusual among the owner-managers I have dealt with in one way: they had begun to make a plan for the next chapter, years before they intended to execute it. From time to time, they asked me to think about what the future might look like without them in the company—in terms of the business model, performance metrics, and organization design. They were driven to make the company as sustainable an organization as possible. Lisa frequently commented: "I didn't spend the best 20 years of my life building an organization to be proud of only to see it shrivel up when Pat and I move on to the next chapter."

One of the moves they made was to recruit and retain a 40-something professional manager, Gunnar Beard, from a European competitor. He took on the role of president. In addition to having a graduate business degree from a top European school, Gunnar had worked for three highly successful European manufacturers, including two that were family controlled. His compensation at TechEdge included incentives based on the increase in enterprise value from the time he entered the business. With this arrangement, Gunnar could look forward to an important payday when a new investor became involved, and he might even have the wherewithal to invest such that he could increase the potential for a future capital gain for himself. So, right from the beginning of Gunnar's relationship with Pat and Lisa, the topic of the best next majority investor was always on the table.

Gunnar was a good fit for TechEdge and for the Snells. Atypically, he was able to take input and coaching from Pat and Lisa without letting it erode his confidence as a professional manager or prevent him from doing what he knew needed to get done. He could see that Pat and Lisa cared about the future of the company and couldn't suppress their caring in the name of objectivity. He approached Bigelow's advisors' engagement with TechEdge with some trepidation at first—after all, life was pretty good with Pat and Lisa as they allowed him to take on more and more responsibility. Gradually, however, he could see that some of the changes he wanted to bring about (such as a more rigorous and specialized global sales management, more plant accountability, and higher hurdles for financial performance—all of which would benefit the company in the long term) would be easier to implement, or might only be possible to implement, after an ownership change. Pat and Lisa had had lots of successes, and it was challenging for them to make the tough decisions about customers and personnel that were needed to get TechEdge to the next stage.

Merritt Capital Partners (MCP), a private equity group, had invested in several companies when it was in the same stage as TechEdge was. The MCP partners were nodding their heads as advisors from my firm explained to them the history and successes of TechEdge and outlined Gunnar's growth plans for the business. The partners offered a competitive economic deal, and their intelligent approach to the negotiation and due diligence process increased our confidence they understood the uniqueness of this family-owned business. When colleagues and I investigated MCP's plans for financing the deal, we learned it intended to have a normal amount of senior debt with a bank and that a small amount (about $15 million) would take the form of a high-coupon subordinated debt. It was going to take half of this in its partnership and outsource half to a small mezzanine lender.

This financing complexity would take some time to work out. When my colleagues and I updated Pat and Lisa about it they responded, "Why don't *we* be the other sub debt lender? If MCP is going to put in $7.5 million, we'll put in $7.5 million as long as we receive the same, identical terms and conditions as MCP. Why wouldn't we? We'll be looking for a way to get some higher income. What better place to put our money than in the company we've been running for the past 20 years—the company that is going to be run by the guy who we hired and trained and trust?"

And that's how the deal was done. Gunnar, still president, has added a plant in Asia, and is now looking for acquisitions.

Bigelow advisors were able to architect an unusual (for a PEG recap) structure for Pat and Lisa, where their reinvestment with the PEG in the new company (called their "rollover") was minimized since Gunnar had the liquidity to invest (because of his unusual comp plan), and MCP really saw it being most important that Gunnar and the half dozen other senior managers had their skin in the game.

Private Equity Platforms: Industry Experience Plus Capital

The third type of investor in the private company transaction market is the private equity platform. This is a hybrid form, with some characteristics of both the strategics and PEGs. Think industry expertise and specialization, powered by the energy of impatient capital.

Platforms used to be rare, but now they are beginning to dominate the space, and that's a good thing for owner-managers.

Private equity platforms are a natural evolution of what the best PEGs have been doing for years: focusing on vertical industries and leveraging that knowledge to increase returns. These groups immerse themselves in certain industries by attending trade shows, targeting potential acquisitions, and hiring experienced operating executives from the industry to help them think through their growth strategies. It works, and investors want more.

The PEG limited partners have played a role in this evolution by pushing their PEG firms to create industry-specific consolidators—platforms—as a way to differentiate their firm from the PEG industry and to earn higher returns. These companies, recapitalized by PEGs, now seek to make acquisitions that strengthen their platform in a specific industry.

By working with a private equity platform, you get some of the benefits of a strategic acquirer, such as management that is experienced and skilled in your vertical industry. You also get a PEG's advantageous financial structure and deal-making speed. Platforms will exit individual businesses just as quickly as PEGs do—sometimes selling the business to another platform, a stand-alone PEG, or to a strategic—but they also have the muscle to propel a successful business into an initial public offering (IPO). Any of these options mean a potential uptick for your 10 to 20 percent equity.

Platforms can be easier for you to deal with than strategics or PEGs are. They speak your language and already know the operational basics of your industry. The dialogue tends to move more quickly into the exciting stuff: the potential for growth and the value of your strategy. At Bigelow, it's unusual for us to invest any time on behalf of a client with any PEG who *hasn't* shown some expertise in a specific industry. Either the group has a platform, or has made a significant investment and is on the way to forming one.

In one regard, platforms operate like PEGs—they acquire 80 to 90 percent of your business, leaving 10 to 20 percent for you and/or your management team, so that you share some of the risk immediately and participate in the gains when they come in the future. And yet, for an owner-manager, success with a platform means opportunity to take advantage of its industry-specific expertise, just as its investors do. At Bigelow, we negotiate for owner-managers to receive their rollover shares in the stock of the *holding company* (the platform), not your specific company. Why shouldn't you have the same synergistic benefits and cost advantages as the platform investors? You're one of them now. Not all PEG platforms readily agree, and that's when it's good to have experienced objective advisors who will advocate for you.

The Family Office

An interesting version of the PEG is a private equity capability of a "family office"—an investment arm of a high-net-worth family that makes direct investments for family members' own accounts. These hybrid PEGs can be an interesting fit for clients for two reasons. First, they are typically successful owner-manager families who have had a wealth creation transaction of their own, so they understand what it's all about. Second, because they are investing their own capital (they don't have to provide a return to anybody but themselves), their time horizon can be infinite, if they are receiving an acceptable return.

Western Foundry Science: A Case for a Platform

Western Foundry Science (WFS), owned by its top three senior owner-managers, is a leading global competitor in the manufacture of critical tolerance parts forged from high-technology materials. The forging industry has bifurcated: there are still some old-fashioned hammer-and-tongs forges out there, but the industry is dominated by plants that, like the one at WFS, look more like high-tech laboratories. The company sells the parts to customers whose products must function flawlessly in a variety of applications for hostile environments, including defense, semiconductor, medical, and commercial aerospace applications.

When I visited WFS's plant I found it to be a marvel. It was completely operated by touch-screen control systems in a plant that looked like an alchemist's laboratory. Proprietary custom-formulated (for the application) molten alloys were being poured white-hot out of a crucible suspended two stories high. Molten metal was sheeting down into custom forms already precisely positioned on automated conveying equipment, which was shuttling them into vacuum ovens for precise heating and cooldown regimens. Open flames leaped on dirt floors surrounded by positive air-pressurized clean rooms, where kitting and assembly might take place after the parts were machined to a rough envelope after they cooled. It was a study in contrasts— space-age technology making ancient alchemy productive.

The owners of WFS were experts in the business, and they had honed their model. They had lived through a period of impersonal, offshore corporate ownership. (They had acquired WFS from the previous corporate owner to save it from the brink of bankruptcy.) They had watched as the former owners devalued the business by focusing solely and heedlessly on building revenue. As a result, these three current owner-managers had become very choosey when it came to taking on new customers. They only took on those customers who desired—indeed *required*—the high-precision tolerances WFS was capable of manufacturing, and who developed mission-critical applications in which the cost of part failure was dramatic, even catastrophic. Their efforts did not go unrewarded. Their customers were willing to pay handsomely for WFS's capability and quality, which enabled WFS to earn an EBITDA that was around twice its industry average.

As my colleagues and I held discussions with some of the best strategic acquirers in the world, it became increasingly clear that Western Foundry Sciences' owner-managers were not enthusiastic about another experience with the bureaucratic economy. All of them had worked for big global companies in the past, and they had survived the politics, the reporting, the focus on quarterly every-thing. They wanted to find a different kind of majority owner, an acquirer that would share their entrepreneurial spirit and "get" the industry they were in. If they could find such an investor, that would be a real win. My colleagues and I spoke with a few PEGs, but they were wary. They considered the foundry business to be a "black art" (nonsystematic and too reliant on the expertise of the individual employees). They were also skittish about environmental issues they assumed would crop up in the plant.

After exploring the universe of the strategic and PEG investors with some rigor, we began a serious negotiation with High Tech Foundry (HTF), a platform investment company of one of the large domestic PEGs. The company was managed by a small team of seasoned industry veterans who had been acquiring other foundry businesses across the United States, all of which served markets adjacent to those of WFS or possessed material science that was incrementally additive. They had a simple business model and a succinct business plan and were diligently focused on executing it. They were acquiring, one after another, adjacent owner-managed companies they believed were a good fit because HTF could bring best practices to WFS and supply them with capital—and these actions would enable the acquired companies to become an integral part of HTF.

The negotiation was short and sweet. High Tech Foundry managers understood the deep know-how that WFS possessed and were not wary of it—they both valued and appreciated it. Nor did they turn away when they discovered that WFS *did* have environmental issues in its manufacturing plant. High Tech Foundry had been through environmental assessment exercises a dozen times before, knew the questions to ask (and the insurance to get), and understood that experience and understanding made life easier on everyone. HTF ended up paying a price that we advisors might have attained from a strategic, with private equity terms. The management team kept a piece of the overall business with the expectation that the holding company might be a candidate for a public offering some day.

The Private Transaction Market: Seller Beware

The stratification of private investors is just one factor that makes the private company transaction market complex, unpredictable, and (seemingly) irrational. Think about it. If you want to know the value of your publicly traded Apple common stock, it's easy: just open your browser, enter AAPL in the appropriate space, and up pops a number. Instantly, you know the value of your shares because the stock trades in an organized regulated market every few seconds. An economist would term the public market *efficient*, in that there is relatively minimal variation around a mean offer.

Most owner-managers are entering the private market for the first (and sometimes last) time. The value of their business is a bit of a mystery to them. Cocktail party talk or country club conversations are confusing, with anecdotes about who sold their business and what they got. But the plural of "anecdote" is not "fact." There are few truly helpful comparisons and, most relevant, *no liquid market* that enables you to sell or buy shares. Unlike the public market, the private market is comparatively inefficient. In other words, there is significant variation around the mean range of offers. And while those offers are not random—they make perfect sense to the offerer's assessment of the enterprise value—they are nowhere near as efficient as the many public market offers on your AAPL stock.

To further complicate matters, owner-managers who enter the private market must deal on the other side of the transaction with coldly objective and experienced investors. Most of them have experience in the private transaction market and perceive themselves to be in a zero-sum game, an "I win when you lose" relationship. This adversarial mindset is not in keeping with the exchange of genuine value these transactions are about, and yet it is there and always influences the game. But it's not a game to you, is it? Not when you've invested so much in building the enterprise value of an organization, and succeeded, maybe beyond what you ever thought possible. That kind of achievement deserves to be rewarded, and when you finally ask, "How much?" the private market answers in its own opaque, inefficient way. It's frustrating.

Let's throw some light on it. Figure 4.2 shows some of our actual "cooking." It represents six actual transactions.

The letters in the left column ("Recent Engagements") represent companies. In the middle, the gray bars represent the range of the offer values, laid out so you can easily see the median offer. The "Sample Size" column gives the number of offers received in that transaction. The right column ("Min/Max Spread") shows the percentage spread between the highest and lowest offers.

So we see that Company A received 10 offers, two from PEGs (boxes), five from strategic investors (triangles), and three from PEG platforms (circles). The median offer for Company A is represented by the vertical line in the middle. Let's say it was $100 million. This diagram informs us that a PEG thought the company was worth

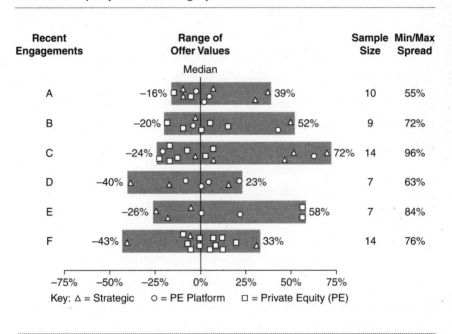

FIGURE 4.2 Understanding the Private Transaction Market—The Private Company Market Is Highly Inefficient, Not Instinctive

$84 million and the high offers—strategics—thought it was worth roughly $139 million. That's a 55 percent variation among some of the most sophisticated and diligent investors in the world. Wow. Possibly it's an anomaly, right? That's what I originally thought when I first started analyzing the variations in transactions.

Now look at the scatter around the median for Companies B, C, D, E, and F. Whoops. No anomalies, just more inefficiency. A strategic investor made the high offer for Company B. It was a Platform that offered the most for Company D, while a strategic offered the least—40 percent lower than the median value. The wide variation of offers and the inconsistency of the type of investor that made the highest and lowest offers continue down the line. I have

117

been analyzing and validating data on private transactions for over a decade. Variations like this are evident on hundreds of other engagements not represented in Figure 4.2 but quite representative of my 30 years of experience in the private market as a whole.

In private transactions, you must *expect* wide variations in offers and then dig into the differing assessments of value. Some patterns reveal themselves. For example, PEGs typically cluster around the mean, and that makes sense. The good people making the offers for the most part went to the same elite schools, studied the same cases, use the same spreadsheets (that they've modeled from one another), and make the same analytical assumptions about the future growth of a business. It would be surprising if their offers did not cluster around the mean.

What else do you see in Figure 4.2? Interestingly, strategic investors seem to fall more frequently in the tails (toward the extremes). In fact, strategics often represent both the highest offers and the lowest offers—*in some cases for the same company.* How can this be? The strategics operate in or around the same industry, right? They have about the same cost of capital. Their management goes to the same trade shows, calls on the same customers, and frequently uses the same suppliers. What are we not understanding about them? What we do not see is the motivation that drives the diverse human beings who are making the offers. They are motivated by knowledge about what their company has baked in its business plan and how this acquisition could help it. Or perhaps they are stimulated by their certainty about where the industry is heading and their belief that this acquisition will get them there quickly. All types of private investors are just humans making their best guesses about the future and translating them into an offer.

The future is not knowable, and a prediction is just a guess in better clothes. Look at the prognosticators of Wall Street or the pundits staring intently at the goings on within the Beltway. None of these people *knows* anything, and yet from their fluff emerges investors' predictions of the future of your enterprise and the price they will pay to own it. They may acquire your business, but they're investing in your future performance, or the future they imagine for it. So, we've got an unknowable (the future) mixed with a variable (multiple predictions of that future) topped off with a squirt of fear ("what if it goes wrong?"). Welcome to the private transaction market. Check your crystal ball at the door.

The Inside View versus the Outside View: The Bias of Inside

Marty and Chris were brothers who owned and operated Porter Co., a distributor of industrial products in the eastern United States. Like many privately owned, experienced niche competitors, they performed well in an industry that was dominated by a handful of publicly owned, multinational behemoths. Over the years, Marty and Chris had dealt with these competitors, keenly competing with them day to day to win and keep customers in the market. And they had run into the owners and managers at various industry activities, including trade shows and golf events, where they would meet their family members and colleagues. Marty and Chris thought they knew their competitor companies well.

When Bigelow was engaged to find the best new majority investor for Porter Co., Marty and Chris had strong feelings about what kind of investors, and which particular ones, would be right to ensure the legacy of the company and would be best for all its stakeholders—employees, customers, and vendors. What's more, Chris and Marty had brought in an outsider, Richard Canning, to become the non-family CEO of the company. The plan was for Rich to continue on with a new owner (Chris and Marty were in their seventies, Rich in his fifties), and Rich echoed Chris and Marty's opinion of the industry players. From their point of view, there were "perfect fits" and "bad guys." To them, the market was so knowable they could practically see the letters of intent in their minds. I wasn't as certain as they were.

As people at Bigelow always do, we brought some alternative options and new faces into the conversation—a mix of PEGs and strategics—but it turns out the keenest interest came from the largest and most dominant company in the industry, "the Big Bad Wolf," as one of the brothers quipped. But he wasn't really joking.

As the engagement went along, four finalists emerged: three strategic investors and a PEG platform. We arranged for each of them to visit the Porter offices, so the management teams could interact and ask detailed questions about the industry they all knew so well. After three of the four meetings had wrapped up, the members of the Porter Co. management team looked glum, even disheartened. Yes, the contenders were all strong, well-managed companies, but they were also loaded down with bureaucratic weight. There was layer upon layer of reporting. MBAs spoke brightly of regular "Friday afternoon check-in meetings." The Porter Co. team felt that if they went with any one of these investors, their days of operating with autonomy were over. Worse yet, the next and final visitor would be the industry leader, the Big Bad Wolf, the company the team expected to hate the most. I could almost see the thought balloons hovering above their heads: *My, what big teeth you have.*

Well, the Wolf turned out to be a whole lot less menacing than anyone expected, including me. Much to Chris and Marty's surprise, the meeting with the management team was completely different than the others had been. While the representatives of the first three bidders had been more polite, less challenging, and presented a less personal, more professional management personality (typical of the bureaucratic economy), they didn't connect with the Porter Co. team in a personal, genuine way.

But in the meeting with the Wolf, the Porter guys learned that, even though the potential acquirer was a multibillion-dollar public company, it was *the only investor whose founder was still the CEO*. The Big Bad Wolf was still controlled and led by its founding owner-manager, and he was very much like Porter Co.'s owners: authentic, direct, candid, transparent, and completely in sync with how the business should be run.

The Wolf, a strategic investor crackling with synergistic opportunities, realized it had found a kindred spirit in Porter Co. and envisioned more clearly (and, as it turned out, more accurately) than any of its competitors what the combination could mean for both companies. My colleagues and I completed a transaction that was great for the families and managers of Porter Co. and at a price that was a high watermark for the industry. Not long after the closing, Richard Canning was named the regional executive of the combined businesses and, under his leadership, they continue to prosper.

Lesson learned. Even in an industry where you think you know everything, you don't know (and neither do I) the true motivations and the relative appeal of one investor over another until advisors have created a competitive market and proactively sought out the best-fit investors. *That's* what the best M&A advisors in the private market do, and they do it very well. Call it being effective within inefficiency. And prepare to be surprised.

Strategics Always Pay More—Until They Don't

There is a narrative fallacy that almost all owner-managers cling to, which is: everyone knows that a strategic buyer will value your company most highly among all buyers. Different versions of this same song are sung in country clubs all across the land. There's only one problem: my experience and scar tissue show it is false. You have seen the data in Figure 4.2. In some cases, strategics do indeed value private companies most highly—when one leverages some of their unique strengths and fits well within the strategic plan they have already adopted. In other cases (actually in most cases), if the business does not fit within their strategic plan, they have *no* interest, and they won't even make an offer.

PEGs and PEG platforms, on the other hand, often offer a wider range of potential growth scenarios, including less conventional ones. They have systematically targeted certain vertical industries in advance, and then seek out companies that fit the targeted industries that meet their criteria for size and financial performance *and* that have management teams they believe can get the company to double its EBITDA in a defined period of time. Other PEGs are less focused by industry and more guided by the gut instinct of their leaders. What gets these folks juiced up is transformative business plans, and some of them have the smarts to know one when they see it. These PEGs can bring big dollars to high-potential ideas.

Case in point: Animal Sciences.

Animal Sciences: Big Dollars for High-Potential Ideas

Animal Sciences manufactures generic pharmaceuticals for use in animal health. When I met them, they were seven years into their venture. The company was started, and funded, by five off-site, equal passive owners (all successful owner-managers in other businesses).

As the Animal Sciences portfolio of commercially accepted animal health pharmaceuticals grew, enterprise value grew as well, reaching several hundreds of millions of dollars—and creating nearly equal amounts of anxiety for the owners. The management team—which also included a smart and seasoned pharmaceutical executive—was less and less comfortable in the weight class they found themselves competing in now. The nonmanaging shareholders were starting to imagine only downside from the dreamed-of enterprise value. The business needed more from the management team than they could execute and more capital than the shareholders could fund. No one had expected the enterprise value of the company to grow so high so quickly. Fortunately, they also sensed it was time to lock in a magnificent capital gain and set the company free to pursue its growth with new investors for whom Animal Sciences would represent a less significant part of their investment portfolio.

That's when Bigelow got the call. We learned from the board that Animal Sciences had endured repeated, persistent, and unsolicited overtures from an international strategic investor that focused on human pharmaceuticals. The would-be investor had been so relentless in his pestering that the board members felt they had been pursued by a marriage suitor. Surely this guy was madly in love with Animal Sciences! Wasn't it obvious that he was the best-fit investor? Didn't it make sense for Bigelow to approach him, close a deal quickly, and be done with it? We advised playing the field.

We spoke with a number of PEGs and strategics and found that both types of investors had a great deal of interest in Animal Sciences. Why wouldn't they? Animal Sciences had proved its competitive advantage, had promising products in the pipeline for approval, and was part of the animal health business that seemed ready to explode—especially for the care of companion animals.

The initial offers came in. After reviewing them, the insistent suitor made it into the final group. The visits from the company's management and their plant tours had gone very well, because as you would expect, the company was a pharmaceutical maker and it knew all about the regulated nature of the business, the good manufacturing practices required to produce good-quality products, and the distribution channels that moved products to market.

When the final offers were due to come in, Bigelow received a phone call from the ebullient president of the pesky pharma suitor. "When my offer letter comes through," he said, "you can turn off your fax machine." (This was a few years ago.) "I have wanted to acquire this company for years, and it is in our strategic plan to be in the animal pharma business now. I love the management team, the product suite, and the locations. I love everything. The board of directors at our parent company in Europe understands our vision and has approved this offer. You will be stunned by it."

The offer came through, and the guy was right, my colleagues and I were stunned. One of our support associates plucked the letter from the fax machine, glanced at the number, and then came striding down the hall, waving the letter over her head, asking brightly, "How much did you guys think the offer on Animal Sciences was going to be?" Everybody looked at her. "Seems awfully low to me," she said as she plopped the letter on the desk.

We were stunned alright. The offer was about 40 percent of the final sell price. Not 40 percent *below* the sell price, 40 percent *of* the sell price. We called the president immediately and asked if he had made a mistake, as we hoped he had: "Did you maybe put the decimal point in the wrong place?" He answered, "I am certain my offer is the best offer you're going to get."

We eventually closed the transaction with one of the best private equity groups in the world—one that had significant experience in animal health—at 2.6 times the offer from the big pharma blusterer. We learned that people from the winning PEG had looked at one important metric, and that is what had decided the issue for them. They asked us this question: "In the human health side of the business, about 80 to 90 percent of the total unit consumption is generics; what is the percentage on the animal side?" We answered, "We believe it's 10 percent." That was really all they needed to know.

Their investment thesis was that generic animal pharmaceuticals would grow to meet or exceed the percentage on the human side. Why wouldn't it? My yellow Labrador Retriever doesn't ask for *Frontline* by name. The new investors saw a transformative opportunity, but the big pharmaceutical strategic was blinded by its own provincial view that the animal health sector couldn't be as valuable as the human health sector.

An important epilogue. The PEG sold Animal Sciences five years later to an international pharmaceutical strategic for a gain that would knock your socks off, and it made another fortune for the management team and founders who reinvested. This goes straight to one of the driving forces in private equity, as well as one of its most stubborn misconceptions: PEGs don't make money by cutting costs; they make it by unleashing long-term value and then by attracting the next investor to that value.

Living in the Tail of the Curve

I have described the differences among these different kinds of investing firms, so now let me talk about some of the similarities. Understand that every global investment firm, no matter what kind it is, is a force to be reckoned with. If the firm has any intelligence at all (and if it is of reasonable size and has succeeded for some period of time, you can be sure it has), and if it has the capital to make a $50 million investment, you must assume it knows what it is doing and knows what you are doing as well. It is not going to get tricked or coerced or "pitched" into becoming your next majority investor. It won't be "sold," believe some clever "spin," or in any way be cajoled. There is no "greater fool theory" today. The best new majority investors have to be individually identified worldwide, rigorously qualified, and then guided through a flexible but structured offering procedure—including the right amount of transparency to make sure they know this is a highly competitive space and low-ball offers won't make it past the recycle bin.

At Bigelow, we work with each client to create competitive anxiety in the minds of the suitors. Our goal is not to get the investor to overpay, yet nothing else but the knowledge that we have created a competitive market will bring out the best fair market value offer. As I've said, we believe that what *you* have to offer is valuable and scarce and that investors need it. For the most part, what investors have to offer is something far less scarce: capital, which—in its old-fashioned form—is green, folds, and has a picture of George Washington on it. *Money is a commodity.* There's plenty of it around, and you can rent it for the same price everywhere.

The art (and science) of M&A advisors' work is to lead investors to the richest possible understanding of your industry, your distinctive strategy within it, your performance, your energy, and your resulting enterprise value. It's the way to bring order to an inefficient market. Because strategic investors and PEGs see different value in similar businesses, there is always going to be a wide variation in how they see the value of your business. Good M&A advisors live in that variation; at Bigelow, we appreciate the perspectives within that variation, and we work to move the entire range right along the axis, pushing the tail farther and farther out until we have confirmed fair market value.

Here's a very rough metaphor. Did you ever sell a piece of residential real estate? Well, your enterprise value is just like a house you love. When you put the house on the market, you say that it is not only the best house on the block but it also is a unique waterfront property and right next to the nature conservancy. There are no other properties like it!

When interested and qualified buyers come in for a viewing of your house, they are almost guaranteed to make offers that cluster around a mean—usually based on the "comparative" sales in the neighborhood, the real estate appraisal, the tax basis, and so on. But you know that you own a *unique* waterfront piece of real estate. There is no comp that is actually comparable.

So what you're looking for in a buyer of that house is not a member of the usual gang of suspects but the one acquirer who says, "*I have to have it.* I have been looking at this property for years. I have always wanted to live here. I never thought it was going to come on the market. And, if it ever did, I didn't think I would have the wherewithal to buy it. But it did, and I do! I don't care what the comps are. They're irrelevant to me." *That's* the investor who pays two standard deviations higher than the mean offer. And that's the one who invests in super landscaping, updates the pool, builds a new dock, and keeps the lawn lights lit. That buyer loves that property, and he or she adds value to it. *That's just the same process you'd use to find the right investor for your enterprise.*

The Dating Game

In the next chapter, I'm going to go deeper into the deliberate and professionally managed process of capturing the value of your enterprise. But let me say a few words about how the process often unfolds before it gets serious and professional—which is in a far less deliberate and transparent fashion. Almost every successful owner-managed firm is, at some point, "approached" by one or more potential investors, both strategics and private equity groups. The contact may be simple and "innocent." The CEO of one of the larger public companies in your market stops by your booth at the industry trade show and invites you out for a beer later. You say, "Sure." If the CEO is sophisticated, he'll tell you how much he admires your product or service—and he'll sincerely mean it.

He'll be courteous, respectful . . . courtly even. He might enviously compare the value you have created within your entrepreneurial economy to rules of the bureaucratic economy he has to contend with. He may advance the idea of working more closely together, or of a strategic alliance where your products or services could be repurposed by his firm. He may say, "Gee, I am going to be in your state next month. I'd love to stop by and say hello while I'm there." The CEO is speaking in code. He is really saying, "Would you be willing to let me bring in my staff to see whether we would like to acquire your firm?"

My advice is to use these advances as learning moments for you and your organization. They give you the opportunity to find out how the big dogs in your industry think. If they ask to look at your financials, should you let them? If they want to meet other members of your organization, should you introduce them? Hell, no. But there is no reason not to conduct an unhurried conversation over a period of months or years that allows you to get to know the big players in your industry. You will learn an incredible amount. They will probably reveal their strategic plans and what their financial goals are. If you ask to talk with a couple of CEOs of companies they have already acquired, it would be unusual if they objected. Why would they? Your purpose in these conversations is to listen, to learn, and to get educated. You can give out a little information, but nothing that would require asking them to sign a confidentiality agreement. Not only are you trying to understand more about the industry, you want to get a sense of whether you even *like* these people. Do they have a philosophy and culture you admire? But understand: from the first sip of that beer after the trade show, the negotiation for your company has begun.

An approach from a PEG will look and feel different from that of a strategic acquirer. People from a PEG are usually a little less courtly.

They tend to think of their attempts to establish a relationship with you as a kind of online dating network for investors. They hire teams of bright, freshly scrubbed undergrads and sit them in front of a computer screen, give them a telephone headset, and set them to work, systematically "dialing for dollars"—calling every company of a specified size in targeted industries or geographic areas. The callers are usually financially incentivized just for getting you to take an initial meeting with the directors of the PEG. The callers are chatty and seemingly knowledgeable about your business. But, as with business brokers looking for listings, conversations with these people are an utter waste of time. Of course, the callers are serious when they say the PEG has an interest in your firm. It has a fund, and the clock is ticking until it has to invest the money or give it back. Of course, the PEG has an interest in *every* successful private company.

Let me repeat: *What you have is inherently valuable and scarce. What investors have is a commodity, and you can rent it at the same price anywhere. What's your big hurry?*

Howard and Alan: What's the Big Hurry?

Howard and Alan Brown were 50–50 partners in Phoenix Precision Products (PPP), a manufacturer of precision parts principally for the "downhole" digital oil and gas business, the oil patch.

I was introduced to Howard and Alan Brown by their tax advisor, a good friend. He called me to ask if I could meet with the Browns on the following Monday—the matter was urgent. It was Friday, and I was in a Florida airport at the time clearing out of the country and headed for the Abacos. I called Alan to see what it was all about. He explained they had a customer coming to visit on Wednesday who they thought might be a key strategic acquirer.

"Let me get this straight," I said. "You have a *customer* who is a potential strategic *acquirer* coming to visit on Wednesday?"

129

"Yes, we do. It's an important customer. Their people broached the acquisition topic with us and asked for a meeting. We weren't sure how to handle it, but we didn't think we could say no."

"What have you shared with them so far?" I asked.

"Oh, they asked for a couple of years of audits, and we sent those off."

"Did you ask them to execute a confidentiality agreement?"

"Ah, no, we didn't think we needed to."

Whoops. After hearing that I said, "Yup, you need an advisor alright." The prospective investor had already begun the negotiation, and Howard and Alan had only begun to realize it. I covered the phone mouthpiece, turned to my wife, and said, "Would you grab our bags off the belt? We have to turn around." Back to the phone. "I'll be there first thing Monday morning."

We had our meeting. We considered the customer, and, surprisingly, it turned out not to be a great fit as a strategic investor. But that Friday morning phone call to the Miami airport sparked a multi-year relationship with Howard and Alan.

When we started talking, Alan was in his early seventies, a patent lawyer by training. He handled some of the selling and administrative functions at PPP. Howard, in his fifties, was the driving force behind the innovation in the plant. He was a gifted technical "tinkerer" in the best sense of the word. In Howard, the company had an unusual combination of the innovator, who produces ideas, and the entrepreneur, who gets things done. Thanks to Howard's efforts, PPP had developed ways to make parts to space shuttle tolerances and work some other kinds of magic that the company's competitors were unable to do. Industry experts have told me that it's because of PPP that the digital oil field exists. Their ingenuity enabled oil and gas explorers to insert navigation devices "down hole" that enable them to drill straight down, move the drill sideways, and continue drilling horizontally for miles. The technique enables the exploration companies to easily and quickly detect where the most fertile energy fields are and thus makes them much more productive.

Over the years, Howard, Alan, and I talked about the ways they could build optimal enterprise value. They leveraged their technical prowess to broaden their customer base in two addressable markets. I helped them to further slice and dice the customer base by industry application, so they could see opportunities to bring more value at a premium price. They started monitoring key industry metrics. They built the next-level management team.

After they had significantly increased their enterprise value, mutually we decided to initiate an engagement where Bigelow would guide them to seek the next majority investor for the company. As with other owner-managers mentioned previously, Howard and Alan had strong notions about many of the potential investors, some of whom were their suppliers or competitors. My colleagues and I spoke to dozens of the best investors worldwide and received some interesting indications of interest. We then held meetings with a large number of interested investors, more of them than we would normally consider to be optimal. We did this because we were sensing that Howard was feeling ambivalent about the whole process, and we wanted to make sure he had several quality investors to choose from.

After the meetings were complete, we picked two finalists and began to negotiate the letter of intent with them. It was then that Howard became increasingly uncomfortable—seemingly with the economic terms and legal conditions. He said he was unimpressed by the enterprise value, although he admitted it was fair market. We almost had to drag him through tedious discussions about legal jargon. He showed a general lack of spirit and enthusiasm. Near the end, he came up with a show-stopping objection. He said he wouldn't agree to indemnify the new owners for claims that might be made by the prior owner. Howard and Alan's attorney patiently explained (once . . . twice . . . many times) that this kind of indemnification was normal, customary, and standard in the market, and the investor had every reason to expect it.

Howard put his foot down. "I can't do it," he said. "I won't do it." We explained the difficulty to the investor. The dialogue came to a screeching halt.

Whoa! When a potential deal is available at market terms and conditions and the owner comes up with an objection like this one, it is usually code. Whether consciously or unconsciously, the owner's code is: "I am not ready for this transition. I'm not sure why. It may be because it's not important enough to me. Or maybe it doesn't feel like it will get me closer to my personal goals. Perhaps I'm just not confident in how things are going."

The morning that Howard said no, he called me and said, "We have to talk." The two of them made the two-hour drive to my office. Howard got right to the point. "Pete, you aren't going to believe this," he said. "I am so sorry. I didn't know this about myself until now. I simply am not going to be able to work for someone else. I thought I could. I thought some of my trepidation would cease once I had the chance to talk with more and more of the investors, but my anxiety actually increased. I now realize I cannot do a transaction with anyone right now, because what all investors naturally have a right to expect—a management team in place enthusiastically ready to do their job—just cannot happen. And we haven't prepared properly with a management team at PPP that can succeed without me. So right now, it isn't as easy as doing the transaction and then having me depart."

My immediate reaction was relief—for Howard. He clearly had been feeling ambivalent for weeks, if not months. From my point of view, I had let him down. I didn't correctly identify his ambivalence and had not surmised his feelings. I never want to be in a position where I am advocating for a transaction that turns out *not* to be what the client wants.

We spent the morning discussing the risks of doing a transaction at that moment and the risks of *not* doing one then. I concluded we had to call off the effort. As soon as we had come to that decision, we knew we had to be transparent and candid with the acquirer and discuss the decision in a fair-minded and collegial way. We needed to get the investor to understand the issues—which were not really about that company or its offer. The ensuing conversations with the potential acquirer were difficult, but ultimately we were able to get them to understand.

There is a happy ending to the story. Two years later, once the management team had been professionalized and augmented, and Bigelow had built a knowledge of PPP, we agreed to execute an expedited engagement process. We spoke with just two potential investors: one PEG, which had not participated in our investor dialogue the first time, and one strategic, which had been the finalist. This time my colleagues and I were able to move from engagement to closing with the chosen investor, the strategic, in just four months—and at a valuation 25 percent higher than it had been two years earlier.

There was also a new and important wrinkle. Through the creative efforts of Howard and Alan's M&A attorney, the team of advisors was able to "carve out" (not sell) a tiny piece of the business that sold tubing products to healthcare applications, which Howard and Alan could run. The operation was not important to the acquirer, and because the deal was presented to people there with this nascent little business already separated out, they had no objections. For Howard and Alan, however, retaining that piece of the business was key. It enabled them to say to themselves, "Well, if all else fails, we still have a business to work on, to grow, and to manage."

Lesson learned: what's your hurry? The personal transition always takes place simultaneously with the professional transaction. Truth serum: if the personal transition goes unaddressed, the owner-manager will begin to consciously or unconsciously find "problems" with the professional deal on the table. He may not even know he's doing it, but he will complain the price is too low, the escrow is too high, the new owner's business plan is no good, the color the owner is going to paint the employee cafeteria is wrong—whatever. He may not realize it, but he's looking for problems with everything because he hasn't addressed the personal issues that are all wrapped up in the professional ones. It's that simple and that complicated. If you cannot articulate your next chapter clearly and with enthusiasm, then it's likely that doing a capital gain transaction immediately is not a good idea.

There is no rush. When the time is right, good advisors will find the investor who genuinely recognizes and is willing to invest in the enterprise you have worked so hard to steward. That one will take care of the management team, build the addition to the plant, expand to new markets, and more. The investor will not only be the best strategic fit, it will also honor your legacy. When it's the right time for you personally and you find that kind of investor, you will not raise objections or try to block the negotiation. You will feel relief, happiness, and optimism for the future—for you and your company.

I have met with hundreds of seasoned, successful owner-managers who, as they approach the mature end of the enterprise arc, begin to ponder their situations as they never have before. No matter how much any of us love what we do or view it as a calling, the demands of the business and its responsibilities eventually cause many to ask, "Who is going to lead this business and assume the responsibility for it after me? Is it fair for me to shuffle the burden for answering this question to the next generation, given the changing industry landscape? Did I sign up for a life sentence?"

This leads to the inevitable questions: "What is the fair market value of my company? Have I created an enterprise with intrinsic value that objective expert investors will appreciate and pay for? What is the market like for my business? Is now the right time to make a move?"

The discussion about the best timing for a value-capturing transaction is usually driven by the owner-manager's sense that the enterprise value is considerable and his feelings of responsibility to preserve that value or to reduce the risk of losing it. Frequently, owner-managers build enterprise value far, far, beyond what their goals ever were and even what they believed they could achieve. As the enterprise value builds and then surpasses a number the owner-manager never thought he or she would reach, let's say $50 million, the conversation tends to go like the one I had with Bill Perkins.

Admissions Software: The Conversation

Bill founded and built a company that grew, over a 10-year period, into the dominant provider of recruiting and admissions software for the education industry. The software helps schools manage the recruiting and admissions process through the techniques of yield management, based on algorithms that take into account enrollment

5

Capturing Enterprise Valu

> There is a tide in the affairs of men which, taken at the
> flood, leads to fortune. Omitted, all the voyages of our
> lives are bound in shallows and in miseries. On such
> a flood sea we are now afloat, and we must take the
> current when it serves—or we may lose our venture.
> —WILLIAM SHAKESPEARE

NOW YOU ARE AT THE MOMENT WHEN YOU FACE SOME OF THE important questions of your business life: "How do I assure the gevity of my enterprise beyond me personally? How will my work be carried on? Who will lead this business when I am around to do so?"

We are all living longer, but none of us are going to live for From a professional point of view, when the discussion of captu enterprise value first comes up, it frequently arises in the context of ing how to pick the next majority owner of the business (after you) example: "How will I find a next majority owner of the business shares some of my principles, who will value and appreciate our cust ers, our employees, all of our other stakeholders, and . . . our legacy capacity, admission scheduling, fields of study, demographics, and many other factors.

As Bill grew the business, he and I would get together once or twice a year. In the beginning, the meetings were held in Bill's garage, which was also the company's headquarters. After a couple of years, we graduated to a closet, and, a few years later, we moved to a glass-walled corner office. Once we had a serious discussion in an airport park 'n' ride where we were both rushing for flights. (We were both busy and in a hurry.) Bill and I discussed all the issues involved in building enterprise value, about the need for working capital, whether to lease or purchase real estate (lease), and when to bring in a sales director from outside the company.

Almost every discussion ended the same way. Bill would look at me quizzically and say, "So, Pete, do you think we're making progress? Given all the hours and sweat I've put in and all the bank loans I've personally guaranteed, do you really think this thing will be worth anything someday? What do you think it's worth now?"

Naturally, my answer varied from year to year. I remember answering that question in succeeding years: "Oh, you're probably in the $10 million range." Then one year, "Maybe $35 million?" In a later year I'd say, "Somewhere in the range of $60 to $80 million."

Bill would nod and go back to work.

Then one year, after a long talk, Bill asked the question again.

"Considering the business backlog," I said, "the flagship names you are landing as clients, and the financial performance you're projecting for this year and next, I'd have to say you're looking at an enterprise value of over $100 million."

"You're kidding," Bill said, with a look of pain and misery on his face. "That is *terrible*."

"Why?" I asked. "I thought you'd be pleased."

"Pete, you don't understand," Bill said. "I could screw it up! I used to know the business inside and out. I knew all about the software code, had relationships with the important customers. I knew the buying criteria. I had my eye on the competitors and understood their strengths and weaknesses. But I don't know any of that stuff today because I've had to turn into a *manager*. If this baby is really worth $100 million, I owe it to my family to take some chips off the table. And for the employees, I should put the company's future into the hands of a majority investor that knows what it's doing. So let's start looking for the next owner of this company *now*."

Bill was now in full loss-aversion mode. His passion to avoid a perceived loss to his theoretical enterprise value exceeded the pleasurable feelings he got from hearing me say his enterprise value had reached $100 million. He turned risk averse, wanting to lock in a gain that he perceived to be a certainty (although of course it wasn't), rather than trying to achieve a marginal enterprise value increase with the possibility of a decline in enterprise value.

The architecture of capturing a capital gain is based on an understanding of the owner-manager's personal and professional objectives. The question, "What does the business need?" gets juxtaposed against, "What do you, as the owner, want to do?" There's a lot at stake: your legacy, name, image, and reputation in the community. No owner-manager wants to be perceived as "selling out." You would not do that.

That's why at Bigelow we ask our owner-manager friends to banish the phrases "selling out" or "selling the company" from their vocabulary. And we ask them to start thinking about how to assure the longevity of their firms (and capture a capital gain they have frequently worked all of their lives to earn) by proactively seeking out and then choosing the next majority owner of the business. Nor do we say that our goal is to "market your business" but rather to "*create* a market *for* your business." The distinction is vitally important to understand and insist upon.

You Need Advice

In my experience, far too many owner-managers, like Bill, approach a company transition with very little understanding of the critical issues involved. As mentioned, the private transaction market today is more complex than ever before. Information and misinformation have never been more available. The private market is populated by three very different kinds of investors, and each one approaches transactions with owner-managers very differently. What's more, even within the categories, the individual firms differ a great deal, one from the other. It's essential that you as owner-manager find the one that will provide the best "fit" for your company—and it stands to reason that once you find the best strategic fit, more often than not you have also found the one investor to whom your firm is worth the most in economic value.

The owner-manager can fall into all kinds of traps when it comes to establishing a dollar value for the company—shooting too high or too low, or basing his or her expectations on personal wishes or the speculations of uninformed outsiders. Remember, almost all owner-managers go through this kind of wealth creation event only once in their life. They are about to embark on the most significant financial event they have ever experienced, never having done it before, unfamiliar with the markets, the players, or even the vocabulary.

As an owner-manager, you are entering your career's largest and most important challenge. It's usually the largest single financial event in your life. Who you pick to become the next majority investor will have great impact on your legacy and the lives of all the stakeholders. It's one you've never done before and may never have another

139

chance to do again. There is no room for "teaching error." Ignorance or inexperience can result in failure—a catastrophic disappointment for you and your stakeholders. Your journey past these challenges will deliver you to a positive and generative legacy: a place where you are rich and enriched, where the ending was made clear in the beginning.

My next suggestion should be obvious: you need advice—expert, experienced advice. (Figure 5.1 illustrates an M&A methodology for engaging expert advice.)

FIGURE 5.1 M&A Methodology—Timing and Sequence Summary

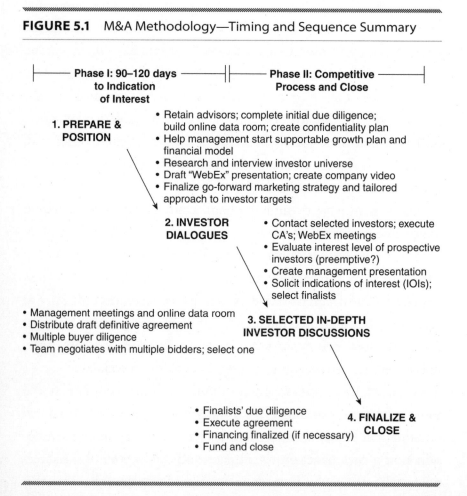

It's not surprising that the words *expert* and *experience* derive from the same Latin root, loosely translated as "to try or test." An expert *has* tried and *been* tested—Ericsson (2006) believes it takes about 10,000 hours of serious practice in a domain to be considered an expert. I'll go further and say that it takes three times that—30,000 hours—to enter the realm of true mastery.

This is not the time for you to try to learn the ropes through trial and error, when your enterprise, its value, and indeed, your life's work are on the line.

There are things you do better than anyone on the planet. And there are things that—forgive me for being candid—you have almost no idea how to do. You know your business, your industry, and your personal goals. You *don't* know how to position and capture the enterprise value you've worked so hard to create. You know your goals but don't know the terrain you will have to traverse to achieve them. It's the same for the best M&A advisors, but reversed. We know the terrain intimately, but we don't know as much as you do about your personal desires and your personal destination. Leveraging the power contained within this asymmetry is what we as genuine expert advisors do.

The two poles of asymmetry are contained in the disparate expertise of principals and advisors.

As a principal, you hold the inside view. You are informed, expert, and biased. You are economically and emotionally invested in the business. You have by far the most at stake in the outcome. You make rational decisions and irrational decisions in equal measure—not good decisions and boneheaded decisions, but rational and irrational as described in the realm of behavioral economics. A rational decision is consistent with your own best interest; an irrational decision is not. As a principal making decisions about your business you are subject to the cognitive biases in your decision making that may

141

lead you astray, which together with M&A advisors you can learn about and guard against.

Your expert advisor's view *must* be coldly objective and unbiased. You don't need to be an ethicist to see that the world is overpopulated with people and companies whose self-interest runs far ahead of yours. World-class advisors are experts in how the longevity of a business is assured through transition to new majority owners. The best advisors are not subject to the psychological biases that act on you as a principal. Their successes and their failures have accumulated into something approaching wisdom. Perhaps "scar tissue" is a better description of what results from this experience, because enduring the process hurts and the eventual healing is evident and leaves them stronger than before.

My mission is to guide owner-managers like you through the simultaneity of the professional transaction and the personal transition. It's the most important professional decision you are likely to ever face. Your family and your heirs are sure sitting at that table too, as is your permanent legacy. It's hard to overstate just how much is on the line. This is certainly no time for an amateur, and not every expert is up to the challenge.

If you do bring an M&A advisor on board and embark on an engagement to seek the next majority owner for your business, realize that you do not have to accept anyone's offer for any reason. And you don't have to define your own success by a wealth creation transaction. You are in the driver's seat, as you always have been.

Knowing Your Own Company

The first step in finding the right-fit investor is for you to understand your own company well, which many owner-managers do not. It's essential to look at your company as outsiders will see it, not as you perceive it. Your advisor can help with this, but, as discussed in Chapter 2, it's also wise to put together a high-functioning advisory board composed of people who represent a variety of perspectives and types of expertise.

When trying to deeply understand your company, the "endowment effect" often kicks in. As mentioned in Chapter 1, this simply means that the owner-manager, because of a lack of knowledge of his own company and its place in the environment, will place a much higher value on the company than the amount he would be willing to pay for the same assets if he were not the owner. So, ownership of an asset endows it, in the owner's eyes, with a value that is probably unrealistically high. When you have an unrealistic idea of your company's worth, it will almost certainly color the conversation you have with potential partners. Too great a focus on economics may make you blind to the other factors and options involved.

My philosophy follows many of the principals of Appreciative Inquiry, a strength-based approach to strategic inquiry and development. This proven model emphasizes organizational assets, distinct capabilities, and superior skills—the foundations of comparative advantage. It's a strategic dialogue, and a very specific one focused on the drivers of enterprise value. Diagnosing and fixing *operational* deficiencies is not on the table or in the toolbox. If the largest challenges are operational, I guide owner-managers to firms that specialize in operations. Strategy is about moving levers to allocate finite resources differently, and one of the most powerful of these is leadership.

As mentioned in Chapter 1, most owner-managers have overwhelmingly superior skills in sales or technology, not management. They love the dance of finding and serving customers, or they love to invent and experiment. What they don't love are traditional management activities, which drain their energy and often render them

143

ineffective (or worse) in those roles. The good news is that many owner-managers understand the gaps in their skills and have balanced them with their own character strengths, usually an uncanny synthesis of authenticity, leadership, fairness, gratitude, and zest. All of these have supported them as they have assembled a talented management team with different, superior skills. It all works . . . until it doesn't.

As the enterprise matures, even a relatively hands-off owner-manager may become immersed in day-to-day management and, to no one's surprise, not do it particularly well. When that happens, communication among the members of the leadership team becomes strained, and decision making devolves into exasperation.

One owner-manager who fits this description said, "My team just doesn't seem to 'get it' anymore." In that specific case, I asked, gently, "Perhaps you are the one who is not 'getting it,' and maybe what the business needs is a new president—a person who could *manage* from the inside, while you, the owner-manager, continue to *lead* from the outside." Strategic conversations like this are often catalysts for a truly objective assessment about the functional organizational structures and how they are (or aren't) evolving in step with the changing realities of an expanding business.

Inside View, Outside View

What do I mean by managing from the inside and leading from the outside?

In every case, without exception, clients I have worked with are the ultimate insiders, the undisputed experts in their industries and their companies. They understand their business model (in some cases they created it), they know where they add real value, and they are aware of where they make the most profit. They know who most of the industry players are, recognize who the good people and bad people are, and understand some of the changing industry dynamics. Their internal expertness shows up in their superior performance compared to others in their industries.

But this inside knowledge, so essential for operating successfully, is also a set of blinders to what is happening on the outside—what's going on with the industry globally, in the context of strategic environmental changes, or relative to all other industries. This is the outside view that your advisor can bring. Advisors look at the situation with the eyes of the objective, outside observers—we see the world the way investors will see the company, industry, and opportunity.

For the advisor, the challenge of finding the best-fit new majority investor is made up of two concurrent (not sequential) efforts: developing the positioning of your company, and at the same time, finding, screening, and qualifying the best new majority investors in the world for your enterprise.

Positioning Your Company to the Private Capital Markets

As described in Chapter 3, there are four important questions that an investor will ask about your company. The first has to do with your industry. So when we advisors think about the positioning of an owner-managed company, we consider a number of industry-related issues. What is the addressable market size? What is its growth rate? What is its attractiveness? Is the industry in or out of favor with institutional investors?

You will have developed answers to these questions as you and your management team have been creating enterprise value (as mentioned in Chapter 3). The goal in this part of the inquiry is to gather and analyze industry data that will enable serious prospective investors to determine, almost at a glance, if they should be interested in your company, and if so, at what value range.

Some industries, and the companies within them, are harder to analyze than others. "Niche" private businesses, which are highly valuable, are frequently challenging to fully understand. In them, the drivers of comparative advantage may not necessarily be obvious. What is the company's business model? What is the greatness that will make the company sustainable for the next owner? These questions will be in the forefront of investors' minds. Your advisor can put the business in its best possible light, helping investors to answer these questions.

Next, advisors think about strategy. What is the client company's strategy, how does that differentiate it from its competition, and is that validated by superior performance relative to the industry? Almost all clients pursue a strategy of differentiation. No client I can think of competes with a low-cost/low-price strategy.

All investors value a business based on what they perceive to be its future—its future growth rate, its future financial performance, its future capital gain value *to them*. Most of the clients I have worked with are focused on the capital gain value of the business, but it's worth remembering that your exit value is the new investors' starting investment level. So where some owner-managers may be somewhat cavalier about metrics such as return on investment (because, after all, their initial financial investment was nearly zero), the next owner's "entry price" is going to be your "exit price," and that owner needs to see how it is going to get a return on investment going forward.

Your M&A advisor should construct an analysis of the value chain in your industry and think about who generates value in it and what that value is, as well as who earns what value in the industry (the two things are not always the same). (See Figure 5.2.) We at Bigelow look hard at the industry landscape and what the channels of distribution are to the customers. We also look at our client's customers and what the business mix is.

FIGURE 5.2 Industry Landscape—U.S. Addressable Market

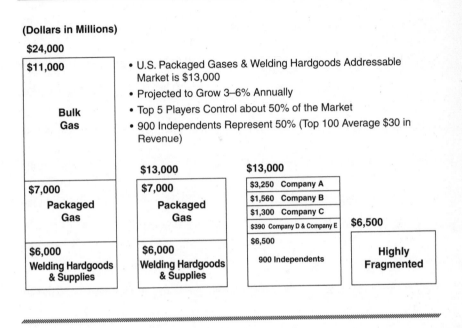

(Dollars in Millions)

- U.S. Packaged Gases & Welding Hardgoods Addressable Market is $13,000
- Projected to Grow 3–6% Annually
- Top 5 Players Control about 50% of the Market
- 900 Independents Represent 50% (Top 100 Average $30 in Revenue)

$24,000
$11,000 — Bulk Gas
$7,000 — Packaged Gas
$6,000 — Welding Hardgoods & Supplies

$13,000
$7,000 — Packaged Gas
$6,000 — Welding Hardgoods & Supplies

$13,000
$3,250 Company A
$1,560 Company B
$1,300 Company C
$390 Company D & Company E
$6,500 — 900 Independents

$6,500 — Highly Fragmented

The analysis is highly industry dependent, but the goal for every client is the same. At Bigelow we want to demonstrate to an investor that our client's company has customers who are important in the industry, that are "sticky" (not likely to move to a different supplier), and that are growing themselves. Ideally, there would not be a lot of customer concentration, because investors (or their banks) tend to view that as risky. (See Figure 5.3.)

Franklin Corporation: Finding a New Market

Every engagement is different. Advisors need to find the right way forward for each client, and sometimes that path is not immediately evident. This was true of Franklin Corporation, one of the largest distributors of animal health supplies in the United States. At first,

FIGURE 5.3   Offerings and Customers—Customer Information

Over 10,300 Active Customer Accounts in 2010

2010E Revenue ($ in Millions)	2010E Revenue	Representative Gross Margin	# of Accounts	Annual Revenue
$15.5	46%	40%	A 106	>$50,000
5.3	16%	50%	B 170	$20,000–$50,000
6.0	18%	55%	C 635	$5,000–$20,000
6.0	18%	65%	D 3,758	$500–$5,000
1.0	3%	75%	D 5,701	$0–$500

advisors at Bigelow scratched our heads about who might be the right-fit strategic investor. There were the usual candidates—one or two worldwide leaders in animal health—who would view Franklin as a "tuck-in." In that kind of transaction, the acquirer "tucks" the acquired company's operations into its main business. Owners are concerned about this strategy, because it typically involves closing physical facilities, laying off people, and changing structures and processes. We also spoke with the best private equity groups in the world. They showed strong interest in Franklin and were willing to pay a premium price and offer other favorable terms and conditions.

But our analysis of the industry prompted us to think *way* outside the box, and that led us to an aha moment. We looked at other supersuccessful distribution companies and realized that distributing supplies to veterinarians was similar in many ways to supplying other kinds of customers, including dentists. Dentists? Yes, dentists and vets share many business characteristics. They work from small offices. They can't plan ahead for their patients' needs and therefore often need quick delivery of supplies, and they are highly surgical and medical supply oriented.

Enter Simpson Dental, a billion-dollar public company value-added distributor of dental supplies, with a high share of the worldwide market of dental supply. It had best-of-class name and reputation, approach to the market, logistics systems, and availability of capital. People at Simpson could see that by bringing Franklin into the fold they could operationalize the skills they had learned in the dental supply industry to the supply industry for vets, which was newer and fast growing. Simpson paid a price that was (and still is) a high–water mark in the industry. In fact, the acquisition turned out to be so transformative the company changed its name from Simpson Dental to Simpson Supply, and the Franklins ran the division for the next five years.

Management Team Engagement

Chapter 4 showed that different kinds of capital providers have different personalities, and—coupled with your personal and professional goals—whichever personality is involved will influence your decision about which members of your management team should be involved in the dialogue. By definition, a strategic investor will evaluate your company in the context of its own strategy—one that is already successful and in place for that organization. It's possible the investor may want to "tuck in" your company. If so, as it already has established senior management, it may not expect anything more from you as owner-manager than to help with the transition. Or, perhaps you may be ready to shove off in your new Oyster 56 yacht for a cruise in the Caribbean followed by the Canal and South

Pacific. In either case, based on your personal goals and intentions, your M&A advisors will help you choose a positioning strategy where it does or does not make sense to feature you personally as the leader, as a manager, or neither. Perhaps a "battlefield promotion" to one or two of your senior management team members is in order. One of them might become president so you can become chairman. When that's the case, you probably should not participate in the investor/management meetings or even meet the investor. Members of the investing company ought to make their investment decision based upon the go-forward management team they'll be working with, and it's in your best interest that they do so.

Many owner-managers are ready to move on to the next chapter in their lives, and the capital gain transaction is a way of successfully concluding the chapter they are in. If you are in that position, it is in your best interest to incentivize your management team with ownership (or the economic value of ownership) as you go through a transaction. Why? First of all, the team will be doing more work than usual. The engagements usually require a substantial amount of management participation in the early stages—to give advisors access to the information they need—and then again at the time of meeting with the investor. In addition to doing this work effectively, members of the management team should communicate their enthusiasm for and commitment to the business, as the financial outcome for the owner-manager can also be dependent on that.

It is critical to understand that the "go-forward plan" is not the M&A advisor's plan; it isn't the exiting owner's plan; it must be the go-forward management team's plan, and team members' credibility is on the line as they advocate for it. It makes sense to align the interest of the owners and the nonowner-management team by using some incentive compensation based upon the transaction closing. In a PEG transaction, this has the additional advantage of giving the management team some liquidity, which they can use to invest in the business going forward. This is an important component to a PEG deal, and it may minimize, or obviate, the need for the exiting stockholders (you) to leave any equity behind, if you prefer not to.

When to Keep Confidential, and When Not To

All my clients are concerned about the highly confidential, even personal, nature of a dialogue that must take place with the prospective investor. And they are right to be. Introducing unnecessary uncertainty into the life of any employee or other stakeholder in an organization is not a sure way to success. So you need to decide when to bring your senior management team and other members of your organization into the dialogue, and the timing of that will depend on the culture of your company.

I have worked with open-book companies (that is, ones who share their financials with all of the employees each month) that have introduced me and my team to the staff at an employee meeting. The owner-manager usually gets up and says, "Look, we are going to seek a new majority investor to bring new energy and capital into the company so we can continue to grow. These people are our M&A advisors. We'll be giving them monthly updates on our performance. You may see them around in the offices or in the plant. Ask them anything you want." This has worked well for the company.

The majority of my clients, however, don't want to reveal anything to the general employee population until they have something *certain* to tell them—what is happening, who the investor is, what the role of the former owners is going to be in the short and long term, and what organizational and compensation/benefit changes are expected, if any. Generally speaking, these clients have been successful in keeping the discussions confidential until they are ready to make an announcement.

For these clients, we at Bigelow do our part in keeping things quiet. After the first visit to a prospective client's headquarters or manufacturing plant, for example, we may hold all subsequent meetings off-site to avoid questions, disruption, or the need for telling "white lies" about who we are and what's going on. Over time, I have come to accept that it's best to keep things confidential as long as doing so is sensible. I am unwilling to tell any tall tales or be disingenuous in any way. I encourage you to do the same. It's one thing to keep the news from the employees until you're really ready to make it public. It's quite another to get into a position where you have to backtrack, deny, or overexplain. Don't go there.

Compartmentalizing and Secrecy

Without a doubt, the issue of confidentiality produces a lot of anxiety for the owner-manager. I've heard this often: "What if my customers hear I am thinking about recapitalizing or choosing a new majority investor? What if my employees think I am selling out? Will my competitors be able to use the rumors and half-truths against me in some way? Pete, you don't understand how small our industry is. It's not like those other industries you work in. Our industry is so small that everyone knows everyone. We have the same customers, go to the same trade shows, use the same vendors and logistics companies. We have to emphasize confidentiality from everyone at all costs, don't we?"

Actually, no. We don't.

It's important to keep in mind that you, the owner-manager, are in control. It's not like the bad old days—before there were private equity groups, PEG platforms, and family offices—when there were only strategic acquirers. In those long-gone times, owner-managers often waited until the very ends of their careers to make a transaction; when they did, they were unprepared for positioning and negotiating, and they were at a severe disadvantage in negotiations with experienced, deep-pocketed strategic acquirers. Often an acquirer only wanted to buy a plant or a capability. For a strategic, the prevailing wisdom was to acquire and integrate as quickly as possible. This was code for layoffs of hourly employees, separations of loyal senior managers, and even a business shutdown and a move of operations to the strategic's headquarters.

Times have changed. It makes no sense to keep your senior management team in the dark once you have decided there will be a capital gain transaction *someday*. Notice I did not say, "Once you have decided to engage an advisor to manage that transaction." The time to bring your senior management team into the discussion about the long-term future of the company is when you have decided there will be a cap gain someday, not at the moment you bring on an advisor. That way, you can be open and honest with your team about your professional goals and how they intersect with your personal goals. It's not like they aren't observing you anyway (and drawing their own conclusions), so you might as well be the one to present the information to them.

I have seen many seasoned, sophisticated owner-managers get this wrong. They behave as if they believe they need to make these decisions alone, usually out of fear. (Fear of what? Failure? Appearing weak? Of being seen as "selling out" or as disloyal?) So they make a mistake—*hear me on this*—a really big mistake, when they send the signal to their management team that they don't respect those managers enough to bring them inside this important discussion.

Some negative-energy people tend to compartmentalize their lives. They live with little candor or transparency with those around them. They keep parts (sometimes big parts) of their lives secret from others, perhaps because they believe that doing so gives them an advantage or leg up on their peers or those around them.

These people often say one thing and do another. They believe they need to act a certain way in order to please others. As a result, they become conflicted and often lose touch with what they really feel, think, and desire in life. They feel increasingly isolated and lonely because they don't want to—or are afraid to—have anyone see who they "really" are. It's likely impossible for them to perform at optimal levels, perform at their best, or be happy in life. They lead lives that are false, shallow, and hollow.

The best owner-managers do not do this. They continually strive for integration in the various aspects of their lives. What they think and say is aligned with what they do and how they act. Being open and truthful gives you the independence to be your genuine self. This increases confidence, security, and simplicity, leading to a life of increased well-being.

My friends, your management teams know who you are. They observe your behavior over a long period of time, sometimes decades. They know how old you are. They have likely watched you evolve from an impetuous seeker of risk to a much more mature, and probably much more risk averse, business owner. They too are thinking about the future of the business and what it means to all of the constituencies. And while they may not have any of their capital at risk, they are invested—heart and soul—in the enterprise too.

I have searched my memory and queried my professional colleagues about this issue, and we all agree. We cannot think of a single instance when an owner-manager shared his private thoughts about the management and ownership transition with his senior management team and there was a bad outcome. We could not think of one business that had been endangered or even an awkward situation that had resulted from such a conversation.

On the other hand, my colleagues and I came up with dozens of anecdotes about owner-managers waiting too long to get their senior teams involved, resulting in a negative outcome. Sometimes they hold off just a little too long, and the result is not much more than bruised feelings characterized by statements like, "I have worked with you for 22 years, and you didn't trust and respect me enough to tell me you met with a strategic investor at the trade show?"

Sometimes, however, the outcome is a lot worse than hurt feelings and outbursts like "If you think I am going to meet with this new investor and sell it on the new business plan that you created without my input, you are very much mistaken. In fact, you should be aware I have no intention of entering into any kind of noncompete agreement with any new investor. And I guess I should tell you I am evaluating my employment options with some of our competitors. They've been romancing me for years, but I ignored them because I hadn't been interested. Until now." Ouch.

Owner-managers who are ill prepared and wait too long to confide in their management teams may find themselves being confronted, sometimes not in a constructive way, with statements such as, "I heard that you're trying to sell the company. Is this true?" Now you're damned if you do and damned if you don't. If you reply, "Yes, I am," the response is sure to be: "Why didn't you trust me enough to tell me?" If you answer, "No, I am not," you have lied. The lie will be discovered the minute you close the deal, if not before.

You have spent many years of your life attracting and retaining the best possible talent. Working alongside them, you've had fun along the way, achieved lots of successes, and created an enterprise with value far in excess of what you dreamed it would be. Why would you do anything to mess up your relationships with the people who are so important to you personally and professionally?

So once you have made the decision that you're going to have a capital gain someday, don't wait. Identify the people who are going to help get you there and, little by little, over time, strategize with them about who the best next majority owner might be. Introduce them to your advisory team. Allow the advisors to educate and bring along the management team as to what to expect in situations like this. Provide them with some kind of economic incentive to help you be successful in finding and closing with a new owner someday.

When you do these things, you're sending positive signals to your management team: "I respect you. I know you are all volunteers here—that is, you could all be working somewhere else. I appreciate you. Your opinions are important to me, and while I am going to make the final decisions on investors, I want your input and will take it into account. I know this is challenging and hard work, and I want to make sure your compensation is aligned with my goals."

The willingness to be vulnerable, to let your thoughts and emotions be accessible to others, is at the core of meaningful human experience. To put your art, ideas, and dreams out into the world—with no assurance of acceptance or appreciation—is to make yourself vulnerable. And by doing that, you show you can be trusted.

You Are Not Looking for a Fool: There Is No Greater Fool Theory

I want to be up front with you and tell you right now there is no way I am going to reveal the recipe to Bigelow's carefully crafted secret sauce—the *how we do* what we do. We have developed it over decades. It's a secret. But I will tell you that in all cases of the *what we do*, we are attempting to find the best investor anywhere in the world who is the best possible big-picture strategic and cultural fit for our client. In so doing, we are finding the investor who most values what the organization is, who most appreciates the position they have built within their industry, and who therefore will most highly value the company.

It is a narrative fallacy of classical economics (by now thoroughly discredited) that there is a "greater fool theory," that somehow advisors are going to find an investor clueless enough to overpay for your company. This is, of course, total nonsense. In the first place, in my experience I wouldn't know how to go about looking for a foolish investor with $50 million or more to spend. Second, none of my clients would want a fool to run the enterprise they have worked so hard to build. Third, I would not want an investor in your company to feel like it had overpaid.

No, the real challenge is to find a few needles in the haystack, a few investors who likely already have it in their business plan to be in your industry and will appreciate the strategic position you have carved out. In more than one case in my experience, my colleagues and I knew we had found the right investors when they asked, "How the heck did you find me, anyway? My board wants us to make acquisitions in this industry, and we had already preliminarily identified the company you represent as one of those we want to speak with." (I gulped and thought to myself: *increase our price expectation!*)

Access to the Same Knowledge

In the search for the best-fit majority owner, we at Bigelow consider thousands of potential investors of all types. We start by looking at summary data, which enables us to understand how these potential investors would view your business. Then, based on our experience and using our judgment, we narrow the list to several dozen candidates. We speak with these potential investors on the phone, taking care not to reveal anything about our client. We ask about their interest in acquisitions and in specific industries, their ability to finance, the outcomes of acquisitions they have made, their approach to management, their concerns, and more.

If potential investors are interested in growing through acquisition, they are more than willing to talk openly with us. They want us to be aware of their business and what they are looking for, in hopes we might "stumble across" an acquisition of interest to them. Of course, we are not in the business of stumbling over anything, but the calls enable us to gather information about these investors that allows us to make a decision about whether to keep them on the list for this particular engagement.

By the end of these conversations, however, private equity groups and strategic investors tend to get a little impatient. They want to know if we are currently representing a specific company and, if so, which one. We, on the other hand, are not inclined to divulge this information, because we are systematically and urgently filtering *in* those investors that we perceive to have the best fit and filtering *out* all the rest of the world.

We narrow the list further and then make our recommendations to our client. The select few investors are then asked to execute a strict confidentiality and nondisclosure agreement. Those who have been filtered out (the majority) never learn the industry our client operates in, the name of the company, or any private information. This is key. We only disclose confidential company information to the few investor candidates we have aggressively filtered in and who have passed all of our (our client's and Bigelow's) mutual criteria. This is different from many other advisory firms that create a prospectus, which contains the company's essential and confidential information, and distribute it widely. They believe that the wider they cast the net, the more likely they will find the right investor for you. We violently disagree with this approach.

FIGURE 5.4 M&A Methodology—The Architecture to Acquire a Best-Fit Investor

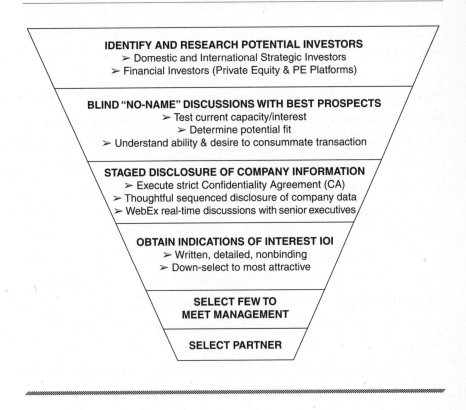

Finding a needle in a haystack is challenging. It takes a kind of detective mentality, as well as a willingness—an *eagerness*—to use technology tools to gather and analyze all kinds of investor information. (See Figure 5.4.) Because we at Bigelow are industry agnostic (we do not favor any particular industry), our broad experience enables us to detect patterns of information in certain industries that look similar to others we have learned about. It also allows us to think creatively about investors who might see high value in your company. On more than one occasion, the discipline of working in several industries at the same time has allowed us to find strategic investors or PEGs who might not otherwise have resulted from an "in-industry" screen. They often had a strategic interest in an opportunity we represented but were not obvious candidates because they weren't in the same industry, operating instead in an adjacent one.

Educating Selected Investors

A traditional M&A advisor's standard practice is to write a prospectus, descriptive informational memorandum, or confidential informational memorandum—whatever they call it. The idea is for the firm to write a "book" that adequately describes your company's unique investment thesis. Then, they hope that investors will take time reading it, make notes about it, and discuss it among themselves at their Monday morning partners meeting. It's a fantasy. The truth is, this is an utterly broken technique, useful in the 1970s perhaps.

We at Bigelow reject the idea of the prospectus and never create one. We know from experience that the key decision makers won't read the book; they'll relegate that boring task to their junior analysts. It sounds illogical, doesn't it? Let the junior analysts decide what investment opportunities the boss gets to look at? Even worse, the prospectus, which contains a great deal of the client company's confidential information, will be stored in the files of the investor firm forever. Yes, the confidentiality/nondisclosure agreement requires the signer to return or destroy copies of the prospectus, but I suspect that if we were to conduct a surprise on-site audit of the acquirer candidates, we might find a few copies of the prospectus lying around.

At Bigelow, we take a different approach. To educate the next investor on your business, we have created a proprietary methodology that uses an online technology-enabled tool. The investors watch a brief slide presentation, with audio, and supported by Web-enabled platforms. This methodology requires that the decision makers from the investor firm (the managing directors from the PEGS; the CEO, CFO and other C-level executives from strategics) join us on the phone and engage in a rich, live presentation followed by a free-flowing dialogue about the important parts of the company to them. Many times, those C-level executives will include senior operating executives in the first meeting, because they want their "combat" input. In those conversations, the investors and the Bigelow team discuss a wide range of issues, including the client company's history, its industry, the addressable market size and growth rate, key players in the market and strategic positioning within the industry, organization and senior management team members, current customers, historical performance metrics, and a glimpse at the future business plan and some future performance metrics. While phone conference attendees engage in this vigorous dialogue, the online tool displays relevant and descriptive graphics, which usually triggers even more dialogue of a very high quality.

The key to the use of this tool in Bigelow's methodology is that it takes place in real time. We get feedback from the decision makers before, during, and after the interactive session. They quickly develop a level of understanding of the business model and the value proposition. The video, images, and graphics enable them to get a detailed picture of the company and the management team. They generally ask highly informed and intelligent questions on topics that are of utmost urgency to them. They frequently ask us to spend extra time on certain specific topics or to skip quickly through others, depending on their own business plan or business strategy. (The nature of their questions also reveals a lot about *them* to us.) Once all the issues have been surfaced and all the questions have been considered, then my colleagues and I are able to have an intelligent conversation with them about their level of interest. In essence, the methodology is a way for us to interview the candidate investors to see if they deserve the opportunity to be the next majority owner of your business. They know that. We haven't distributed a book to everyone, hoping someone will respond. The negotiation has already begun, and we have the right people at the table.

Indications of Interest

Once we have completed the education process, Bigelow requires the investors to specify their level of interest in your business with a written document known as an indication of interest (IOI). This is a written, detailed, but nonbinding offer for the company that outlines the investors' economic interest in your company, a valuation range, and an explanation of how that range has been determined. The document specifies the investor's sources and uses of funds (including financing needs, if any), includes preliminary views to seller indemnity, outlines questions the investor might have, describes the investor's intentions toward management, and mentions contingencies, a timetable, and a work plan. Bigelow IOIs frequently ask for a level of detail that others do not. We do this because at this point in the negotiation (which has already started) *you, our client, have the most leverage.* The investors know my colleagues and I are talking with more than one of them. Their competitive anxiety, their fear of loss, will bring out fair market terms and conditions. We want them to tell us what sort of detailed indemnities, terms, escrows, and other specifics they usually ask for. They might argue they haven't had an opportunity to do their business investigation yet—which is true. If they were to discover something in their due diligence business investigation that was truly a surprise or mistakenly misrepresented by us or our client, then we would consider a definitive agreement that is different from the IOI. Nevertheless, *this is our time* to gather, study, and screen the investors who have seen the preliminary

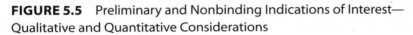

FIGURE 5.5 Preliminary and Nonbinding Indications of Interest—Qualitative and Quantitative Considerations

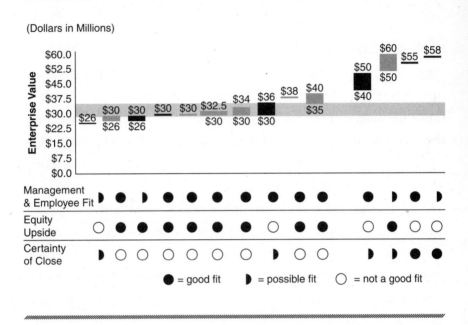

information on the company and to decide which ones (if any) to move into the next stage.

To analyze the IOIs, we at Bigelow prepare an analysis grid like the one shown in Figure 5.5. It doesn't capture all of the qualitative differences among the offers, but it provides enough of a useful apples-to-apples comparison that one or two preferred investors often stand out. My colleagues and I also have probing discussions with the investors who submitted IOIs to ensure we understand their offers completely. The combination of the IOI grid and these discussions almost always enables us to identify a couple of preferred investors. We might then have further dialogue with them, or we might ask them to improve their offer in some way (not always financially), before selecting a few to meet the management team.

163

Investor Management Meetings

Now come the meetings of the management team with a few chosen investors.

Up to this point, the investors have only been talking with us at Bigelow. They haven't visited your location or met with you or your management team. The Web-enabled presentation has given the investors plenty of history on your company, but now they want to talk about the future. They need to evaluate your vision and assess their own ability to execute a go-forward plan that will double the EBITDA of the business over the next five years—from organic growth and without further acquisitions.

Few management teams have experience with and are accustomed to presenting the "whole business" to outside investors, who, as I've said, tend to be coldly objective and highly analytical in their approach. My colleagues and I work hard to prepare our clients for these meetings. We don't and cannot develop a script that you have to follow. We just try to anticipate the kinds of questions investors will ask and rehearse them with you and the management team so you are as well prepared as possible.

The good news is that slicing and dicing the business from an outside view is usually incredibly enlightening to the management team. It's unlikely team members have looked at their business in this way before. They rarely get the opportunity to hear their peers make a presentation about their particular functional domain in the business. After these meetings, owners are often wowed by how passionately and expertly the management team members have presented the company and tell us how proud they felt. Management teams often remark that preparing for and going through the management meetings has been valuable to them as individuals and for the company—even if the process did not proceed to a transaction.

Confidential Information in a Cloud-Based Data Room

From the first meeting with a prospective client, we at Bigelow create and update the information we receive from the company—including all contracts and other legal documents as well as the various analyses that we perform. These files cover a lot of territory, including some information you may not be keen on sharing with others, such as unfunded pension obligations, concerns about environmental claims, threatened lawsuits, and product liability claims.

Bigelow's approach is to disclose your information as early as possible in the dialogue with the preferred investor candidates. Usually that will be after the management meetings when my colleagues and I will invite one or two of the investors to move from IOI to a full-fledged letter of intent (LOI) with a markup of a stock purchase agreement (or asset purchase agreement) that has been drafted by your M&A legal counsel. From the first time we meet with a prospective client, we have been creating and updating these electronic files on all of the information we receive from the company and the various analyses that we perform. This includes all contracts and other legal docs.

This procedure is very different from the "bad old days" when the investor only got a look at your information after making an offer that was accepted. Then the investor deployed a squad of attorneys and accountants to pore through "bankers' boxes" crammed with paper files and dispatched still more representatives to visit the company. There they would spend days, sometimes weeks or even months, reviewing accounting and operational records as part of their business "due diligence" review.

Today, all of these documents are stored electronically in a secure, cloud-based data room that is administered by a third party. At Bigelow, we work with our clients to specify who will have access to the data room and what privileges they will have once they enter—which documents they can view, download, print, or share. And, of course, we can track all activity in the data room. There is radical transparency plus complete confidentiality.

With this approach, the investor candidate does not need to spend any time on the company's premises, except for a plant tour. It does not need to devote lots of time and resource to handling paper documents. It does not have to wait until *after* a letter of intent is accepted to conduct its due diligence. It can get started when the LOI is offered, so all of the pertinent information (including any information the investor might consider to be disappointing) is taken into account in the LOI.

This level of up-front disclosure is not customary in the M&A profession. Why do we at Bigelow consider it so important? Because the LOI usually contains an exclusivity provision that specifies that our client must not initiate contact with any new investor candidates and prohibits them from engaging in further discussions with investors they have already met. When the investor is freed from that competitive threat, the leverage of the negotiation subtly shifts to them. That's why we want to get all the information out in the open and the economic and noneconomic terms fully negotiated before we lose that advantage.

The Letter of Intent and the Markup of the Definitive Agreement

Once the management meetings have concluded, everybody has a pretty good idea of how the investors compare on the qualitative criteria. Frequently, one investor group rises to the top, both in qualitative and quantitative terms, and it's obvious that's the one we want—but sometimes there are two or three still in the game. If there is a single winner, we will proceed to a definitive agreement. If we agree that we'd like to see final terms from more than one investor, we ask each for a letter of intent.

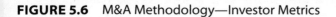

FIGURE 5.6   M&A Methodology—Investor Metrics

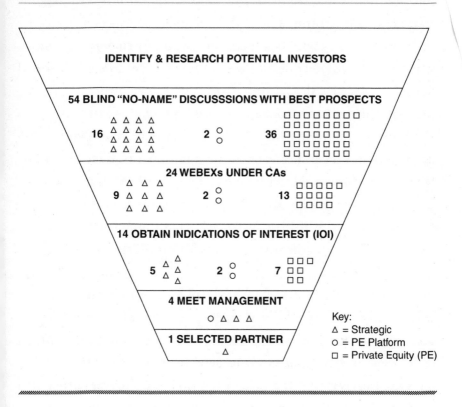

A Final Word about Enterprise Value

What's the asking price?

Warren Buffett says you should not bother calling him about acquiring your business if you don't have an asking price. Well, I guess that means none of Bigelow's client businesses will ever be acquired by Berkshire Hathaway, because we never put an asking price on the table. I think everybody would agree that Buffett is a great investor. Do you think he buys companies at the highest possible prices? Do you think he has an asking price when he goes to *sell* one of his businesses? The answers are no and no. Buffett wants the

Whether the transaction involves a stock purchase agreemen an asset purchase agreement, my colleagues and I usually recc mend that your attorneys draft the document and present it to investors for their review and markup. The draft sets forth the te that have been agreed to and is usually fairly middle-of-the-r or even relatively seller friendly. This is where the experience o M&A special counsel comes in particularly handy.

I want to emphasize that Bigelow's philosophy during the en negotiation is very different from the traditional view. It used to that M&A advisors went hat in hand to the investor commur showed them a description of the client's business, and hoped one of them would "like" it. What they had (capital) was desira and what M&A advisors represented (a private company) seemed in demand.

Our approach at Bigelow turns the old way upside down. To what our clients possess is a scarce and valuable item: a su successful, private, owner-managed business that is highly val by its constituencies and validated by achieving performance at the industry average. The investor groups are the ones offeri commodity: capital. Currently there are over two thousand P] in the world, and the alternative assets data and intelligence Preqin estimates that they have raised over $500 billion more t they have invested.

So my colleagues and I, unlike other M&A advisors, no lo approach potential new majority investors with hat in hand. Figure 5.6.) On the contrary, *we interview them*, challenging the prove to us (through their actions, words, and economic offer) they are worthy of owning the entity you have stewarded for so l possess the wherewithal to deliver the capital gain you have wo your life to build, and have the capability to assure the longevit your company.

owner-managers of businesses he might acquire to have an asking price because it has the very convenient effect (for him) of capping the potential enterprise value. (Anchoring bias sets in.)

My colleagues and I cannot know the business plans of an *acquirer* intimately enough to ascertain what the asking price for a particular business should be for that prospective investor. We may use a psychological anchor or suggest a floor price when we explain to a prospective investor that there is no way our client will consider an offer below a certain level. Companies are not like real estate, where the selling price of similar properties in the same area can be used as comparison. An owner-managed business is more like a piece of art in the way that an acquirer values it. A large part of the valuation is based on the psychology of the investor and his views on scarcity and value. If we suggest an anchor value, either overtly or by metaphor (obviously a high one), the effect is to indicate that we believe our client's enterprise is highly valuable and to imply that we are talking with *other* prospective investors who think the same way.

There is no quantitative way to determine how skillful (or artful) an M&A advisor is in achieving high valuations for its clients. The best data we at Bigelow have seen—and we judge ourselves in light of it—is the enterprise value compared to the standard multiple of the industry our client is in. For example, if our client is in the commercial printing business where (as of this writing) the multiples are low, about 4 times EBITDA, then we would feel happy for our client if we were able to achieve a 6 times multiple (a 50 percent premium to the industry). But we don't feel so great if we achieve an 8½ times multiple in an industry that is currently selling for 9. That's why we urge you to steer clear of cocktail party chatter about your neighbor's multiple. The multiple of anecdote is not expertise. Averages obscure reality. The enterprise value must be judged in the context of the industry.

Leave Some Chocolates in the Box

Let me close this chapter with a story that I hope provides some perspective on price and value.

Harry Cohen's company was one of the largest and most successful distributors of stainless steel tubing on the planet. Harry grew up in Brockton, a working-class city near Boston, where his father was a scrap metal dealer who bought unsorted metal scrap and resold it in large lots. Harry and his wife, Rosa—who managed the books and customer relationships—had transformed the company into a commodities trader that also distributed stainless steel tubing. Harry was a down-to-earth business leader, a trader extraordinaire, and he had grown the business to be worth tens of millions of dollars. When the company reached a certain size, Rosa decided that she no longer had the expertise needed to do the job, and she left the company to pursue her own interests in the community. She looked forward to the day when Harry would do the same.

Harry saw that, although the operation was thriving, there was disruption on the horizon. He believed the industry was moving toward vertical consolidation, where the mining companies would acquire the mills, and the mills would acquire the distributors, which would mean that the smart mining companies would be on the lookout, sooner rather than later, for a strong distribution company. Maybe this would be a good time for an exit.

In due time, my colleagues and I at Bigelow, working with Harry and his team, began to seek companies that could become the next majority owner of the business. Ultimately we closed a transaction with Canalloy, a global company headquartered in Canada.

The transaction included a major capital gain for Harry, Rosa, and other members of his family, and the story of how we arrived at the number is instructive—especially because the figure might have been more. The scene was our offices. Harry and I were meeting with two of Canalloy's senior officers. They knew very well that we were evaluating a number of offers in addition to their own. The sun was beaming in through the glass walls of the pristine conference room that afternoon, but the air was heavy with competitive anxiety, making the Canalloy people pleasantly agreeable on price and other terms. There was a final number on the table, and the negotiations were deep into the noneconomic terms and conditions that ultimately would affect whether or not this transaction was good for Harry and his family. We were close, but I thought we could do better. I called for a timeout.

Harry and I walked down the hall for a cup of java. "What are you doing, Peetah?" he bellowed in his Boston accent. "We have 'em right where we want 'em, let's get 'em to sign!"

"Harry, my intuition and experience are screaming at me. Since we started negotiating with these people, the price of commodities has jumped, and your financial performance has too. If we throw the competitive card on the table, we will likely get a 10 percent price increase."

Harry was surprised, "Whoa, 10 percent? That's big money."

"Yup, it is, Harry," I said. "I would guess that they will expect us to ask for more, and could agree to it this afternoon. But if they won't, let's adjourn. Let them think about it for a few days."

Harry wasn't buying it.

"Are you nuts?" Harry asked. "These guys are ready to sign. The price is way higher than either of us expected and you want to let them walk?"

"Not walk forever . . ."

Harry cut me off. "Let me ask you a question, Pete. What is the probability we get the 10 percent price increase?"

"Maybe 50 percent this afternoon. Ultimately, 80 percent."

"And what do you think the probability is they walk forever?"

"Maybe 20 percent."

Harry thought for a moment, played with his wedding ring, and probably thought about what Rosa would say if he shunned the current offer. He snapped to a decision. "Let's go back in there, tell 'em they have a deal, and shake hands. This is a good deal for them and a good deal for us."

I drew a breath for one more run at the argument, but Harry's mind was made up.

"We want them to appreciate this business—to take care of it. I'm sure that between now and the closing, they will find some things about us that aren't perfect," Harry said. "And when they do, I want 'em to remember that they got a good deal—*not* that we squeezed the last 10 percent out of 'em."

He finished his speech with a line that has become part of the Bigelow lore.

"So let's leave a few chocolates in the box of candy they're buying from us."

I tell this story not to illustrate a negotiation strategy or to recommend that the owner-manager settle for a reduced enterprise value. Harry's story is a tale of character and virtue and a demonstration that the selling price is important but it isn't everything.

Character, legacy, sustainability, good relationships, and a feeling of ensuring the long-term prosperity of the company—owner-managers value all these things as highly as they do their ability to buy another home or to support another charity.

So think about leaving a few chocolates in the box. It will help when you move on to the next stage, which can be the toughest of all: making the transition into the next step of the arc.

6

Creating a Positive Legacy

Gold is good only for filling teeth and gilding picture frames.
The fun is in the striving not the arriving. Money earned
is of no use until it is usefully invested or given away.
—ROGER W. BABSON

NOW WE COME TO THE STAGE OF THE VALUE-CAPTURE EVENT THAT is rarely discussed and often completely ignored in the company transaction: your next chapter. For the owner-manager, the years immediately following a wealth creation transaction constitute uncharted territory and are unexpectedly challenging personally. He or she arrives at the doorstep to the future, with a pile of liquidity to put to work, but usually no plan—or the sketchiest of plans for the years ahead.

Over the years, I have found that what happens to the individual, the family, and the company after the transaction is just as important—in many cases, it's more important—as what takes place in the transaction event itself. After all, the point of the wealth creation transaction is to get you closer to your personal goals and desired destination. And no matter how brilliant, well read, or thoughtful the owner-managers may be, I have found that in every case—without exception—they are surprised by just how challenging it is to move from being the leader of a business to the next stage of their lives.

To achieve the best outcome, you as owner-manager will have to ask and answer some tough questions about your evolving role in your business and how your personal identity is wrapped up in it. It means imagining what life will really be like on the first Monday after the closing. It involves imagining the lives of your customers, vendors, and employees; of your partners and your family; and of you and your spouse after the new owners are driving the vehicle that you toiled over for so long. It requires learning about how you might manage the newly liquid wealth that will be created in a transaction someday. It also encompasses thinking about and exploring a new life purpose or, at the very least, a changed role in the enterprise. Can you imagine it?

Do You Really Want to Achieve a Wealth Creation Event?

At some point, in building your company, you find yourself wondering: *Hmm . . . will I* ever *get this business to achieve a wealth creation event someday? It sure would be nice to think that the passion, effort, and sweat—not to mention the cash—that I have been pouring into this business would result in a capital gain where I could get some serious chips off the table someday. Now, that would be a great goal to achieve, wouldn't it?*

Or would it? For seasoned, successful owner-managers, the fun and flourishing in life has always come from striving for goals more than achieving them. After they go through a successful wealth creation transaction, what goals do they have then? What should they strive for? Look again at Figure 2.2. On that graph, can the entrepreneur's life arc possibly swoop up from the point where he or she achieves a wealth-building transaction to a whole new level of achievement? Almost no friend or client of mine has ever really understood in advance just how much upheaval, sense of loss of purpose, change in role, and loss of identity is involved. And the identity change isn't usually merely the owner-manager's—it's the entire family's as well. Their whole community of relationships changes, the ones they have been building and taking care of for the last several decades. It's worth thinking deeply about these issues now. It's hard work and challenging. But there is no doubt it's worth the investment to be radically honest with yourself now to think through these issues that will affect the future quality of your long life ahead. In my experience, for an owner-manager to have a successful capital gain transaction he must have clarity on what he will be striving for, personally and professionally, in the next chapter. Why? Precisely because if the capital gain is the end of the striving, then it could also be the end of fun, indeed the end of happiness. That's why it's so important that the transaction has to be seen as the end of one chapter of striving. Now the (former) owner-manager must place his attention and throw his energy into the next chapter of striving for purpose and meaning.

Assessing the Limits of Your Inspiring Leadership: Your Performance Will Regress to the Mean

When should you begin thinking seriously about the transition?

From the very beginning.

That's because a chief executive officer's decline almost always begins during the most successful period of his business life.[1] Even as the accomplishments mount up, he becomes increasingly preoccupied with thoughts about the transition, which he sees as the final test of his stewardship. It becomes more and more difficult for him to think clearly and to make sound decisions.

Ever watch a star athlete try to compete for a couple of years too long? Ever see a baseball manager who should have hung up his cleats at the end of the last season?

There are many factors that contribute to the decline of the CEO's effectiveness as he thinks about the next chapter. For one, the environment in which he operates has changed dramatically. When the owner-manager entered the business some 30 years ago, the landscape was relatively stable and predictable; today we all live with constant change, which takes place at a pace and to an extent never before experienced. Market shifts, both threatening and encouraging, loom everywhere. No wonder the CEO becomes preoccupied. What awaits the business in the years ahead?

The desires, goals, and attitudes of the extended management "family" also come into play when you begin to think about the transition. Over the years, the management family has shared your passion and mission and helped create an operating culture that has produced outstanding results. The business has grown and grown. With good luck falling upon great talent, stockholder value has increased dramatically—frequently, far beyond what you, and they, ever imagined. But during a time of peak performance and great success, the gratitude of the business family begins to shift. You begin to want to protect the business more than they want to grow and build it further. Your team senses this wish for protection. And this attitude accelerates the decline of the CEO.

During this period, people may begin to notice a personality change. You may become abrupt, preoccupied, risk averse. To some people you might seem depressed. You're distracted in meetings and in phone conversations with insiders and with customers too. You attempt to give more responsibility for critical decisions to the team. But you're not convincing. The team may come to understand that your behavior and actions are symptoms of the owner-CEO who has stayed too long.

Knowing that you can't express your concerns and fears to anyone inside the company, you look to outsiders for help: your accountant, your lawyer, a personal coach, or the members of your forum group. All the while, you're engaging in a debate with yourself. Evidently many CEOs are poor students of probability theory. Performance naturally regresses to the mean. Your rational brain urgently whispers, "Transition out, you are holding the company back!" But that ancient, limbic portion of your brain is still churning with greed and a desire for never-ending power.

The challenge is to know yourself well enough so you can overcome the powerful call of the ancient limbic brain. You have to find the strength and wisdom to acknowledge the consequences that good luck has visited on your skill and initiate the transition with the same energy that enabled you to launch your outstanding business way back when. Are humans skilled at knowing ourselves well enough to overcome the ancient limbic brain? Do we dare acknowledge the consequences of good luck visited on our skill, and initiate needed management and ownership transition with the same energy that launched an outstanding business 30 short years ago?[2]

An Exercise by the Fire

Sometimes a simple exercise with a friend can help this thought process along.

The need to visualize a new future was exactly the issue for Steve Pawlak and his wife, Jen. They had been married for over 30 years and owned a highly successful CEO executive coaching business based in the United States, with six offices around the world. They

177

were the parents of two sons. One was working in the company with modest success, but the Pawlaks didn't want to saddle him with the responsibility of leading the company in the future. The other son was learning disabled, although highly functioning, and he came to work with them every day because it was a "safe place" for him to be. The need to provide for his financial security was always in the couple's thoughts.

We at Bigelow had been working with the Pawlaks for some time to find the best way forward for them and their business. The process had just begun, and everything was on the table—a recapitalization, a deal with a strategic acquirer, or a private equity transaction.

At that time, Steve—who was the founder, chief rainmaker, and relationship leader for the most important clients—was in his early sixties and throughout his entire working life had managed to completely avoid thinking about the next chapter. The company had been spectacularly successful, and during those times of peak performance, Steve had begun the inevitable decline as CEO that I have described. Now he began to really understand that, whatever the nature of the transaction, his role would have to change. He might like to stay on for some time as CEO or in another management position. He might consult to the company. He might leave altogether. He hadn't thought it through. He just wasn't sure. The business was a big part of his sense of self-meaning and identity—both for himself and for his family. And how might his role with his wife and his family change if he were no longer focused on the business 24/7?

Steve tried to think through all his options by himself. He couldn't discuss the issues with his management team, and he did not have people outside the company whom he thought he could trust with this issue. Finally he realized that he just wasn't wired in a way that enabled him to conceptualize a future without a company, and he asked if I could help. Building on some of the foundational ideas of my friend Dan Sullivan, I put together a simple thought experiment for Steve and Jen to do together. We gathered at their impeccable, antique-filled colonial home one evening and settled ourselves by a crackling fire.

"All you have to do," I said, "is answer the following two questions."

Steve looked at me blankly. He had no idea what was in store for him. He wasn't particularly fond of this kind of vague, qualitative exercise—even though his whole business was built around executive coaching.

"The first question is this," I said. "Let's pretend that you go to sleep tonight, wake up tomorrow, and, magically, it's actually three years from now."

Steve made a dismissive kind of noise.

"Stay with me, Steve," I said looking him directly in the eye. "For you to feel overwhelmingly successful three years out, what would have had to happen to the business?"

"What would have had to happen?" Steve asked.

"Yes. What would the business look like? How would the organization be structured? How many people would work there? How profitable would it be? What new markets or products might you be invested in? How would the reputation and image of the business have evolved? Who would be leading the company? Steve, what would your role be? Jen, what about yours?"

"That's more than one question," Steve said.

"And here comes the second one," I said. "Now answer the same question for you personally. You go to sleep tonight, and when you wake up, magically, it's three years from today. What would have had to happen in that time that would make you feel those years had been overwhelmingly successful? What would you be working on?

Where would you be spending your time and energy? Where would you be living?"

"Well . . . " Steve began.

"I'd like you to write out the answers," I said. I used the three-year time frame because I thought it was long enough to transcend day-to-day operating issues but still short enough to imagine in detail (unlike, say, five years). I placed Steve and Jen in the future looking back over their shoulders, not wishfully imagining what they could have done but looking back upon what they actually did accomplish professionally and personally in that time. The questions I asked evoked the positive feelings and emotions they had as they looked back on what they accomplished.

Steve and Jen spent about 30 minutes writing, and then I asked each one to read his and her answers aloud. All of us were astonished by what we heard. Both of them said they wanted to be free of all their day-to-day responsibilities with the company. They saw themselves living in a new location, maybe in a sunnier spot, maybe closer to their son, who was based in another part of the United States, or possibly even in another country. They pictured themselves devoting a lot of time to family matters and to the many charitable activities they were already engaged with. The financial security for their learning-disabled son was assured, and they would be able to take care of him not only as long as they lived but perhaps for his entire life through guardians they could identify, get to know, and work with now. They also wanted to travel. And Steve thought it might be fun to get back to one-on-one coaching for a few select clients—when he felt like it.

One of the most important outcomes of the exercise was that it forced Steve to think through what his role in the business meant to him personally—as a successful individual. Like most other successful owner-managers, his concept of life purpose, personal identity, and sense of self-worth was consciously or unconsciously all tied up with the business. He wasn't at all sure he would "like" being anything but the leader of the firm.

From Steve and Jen's answers to my questions, however, it had become much clearer what the general nature of the transaction should be. Still, it took a lot more dialogue over a period of months—with Steve, Jen, the Pawlaks' sons, the business's management team and advisors, and me—to nail down the details. We ultimately did accomplish a modest recapitalization transaction with a high-net-worth individual who became a minority shareholder, and that transaction served as a "down-payment" step toward an ownership and management succession.

Three years later, Steve and Jen were living a life that was a lot closer to the one they had imagined. Thanks to a combination of blue-sky thinking and down-to-earth planning, they were able to look at their lives and their company and feel that both were a success.

Some time later, Jen told me that the evening we had spent by the fire thinking about personal goals had been one of the most clarifying events in their lives together.

I suggest you try this quick thought exercise for yourself. You go to sleep, wake up tomorrow, and magically it is three years in the future. Think about your life the last three years and imagine that they were the best three years for you professionally and personally. Can you graphically and colorfully describe what took place? Think through this question: if the "striving" in the current business is completed and the acquisition of the next majority investor is successful, then what are the new personal or new professional goals you will be striving for?

In finance, the difference between the future value and the present value is known as "discount." In psychology, the difference between where you are today in your life compared to where you ideally want to be is called "discrepancy." Regardless of whether you think in terms of discount or discrepancy, have you invested the needed energy and time to think through what your "next chapter" looks like?

The Four Posttransaction Stages

In my experience, almost all owner-managers seriously underestimate the disruption to their lives that a wealth creation event will cause. They have never done this before, and naturally, because of their positive nature, they expect they will be able to manage it. But they often struggle with it, because this new chapter of life is so different from anything they've done before.

In an instant, the owner-managers are going to lose at least one and usually two of the four roles—CEO and owner—that they have been playing for many years. This puts them in a new and often unsettling position. In the CEO and owner roles, they prided themselves on their ability to deal with conflict and manage complexity, and now—as family members and individuals—life is often simpler and the conflicts are of a very different kind and possibly less energizing.

To make matters more complicated, some of the same decision-making behaviors and thinking biases that may have come into play while running the business will still be there when considering the next step. Why wouldn't they?

So the owner-managers need to learn how to think about a future that does not revolve around building a company. It may mean doing some dreaming and imagining of the kind the Pawlaks did. It may also involve practical planning and hardheaded decision making, almost like any other business activity.

The Four Stages of Personal Transition

It's useful to set goals and to consider where you'd like to be in three years, but, as with any plan, personal or professional, rarely does the execution go as smoothly or as uneventfully as one might expect. We at Bigelow have found that an owner-manager typically progresses through four stages after a transaction. Knowing what they are and understanding what each involves can make the outcome much more positive.

My colleagues and I can predict these steps with great precision because we have observed our best friends and clients go through them over the past 30 years. Sure, the best owner-managers prepare in advance, and some are agile enough to prepare along the way. The distracted ones prepare after the closing but—*hear me on this*— virtually every seasoned, successful owner-manager I have ever met is shocked by how challenging it is. You can prepare in advance or just let it happen to you, but there is going to be a mammoth personal transition in your life as your professional transaction comes to successful completion.

Stage 1: Realization

Ideally, this first stage ought to begin before the wealth creation event and even before a new majority investor or a recapitalization is sought, but it rarely does. It starts with the realization of the simultaneity of the personal transition and professional transaction.

Time stops. Even brilliant owner-managers underestimate the hard work of anticipating the cultural and psychological changes they will be encountering. One recently said to me, "I didn't know how good my company was until I sold it. Now what? Sure, I can go play as much golf as I want. But I'm 50, and all my golf buddies have jobs. What am I going to do, play by myself?" Whoa!

You as owner-manager probably have a lot of fun working, and if the next chapter calls for you to "retire," you will miss that. You are industrious and are good at work; you may or may not be as good at "active leisure." Many of us seem more wired to achieve. Your journey to fortune and legacy, after all, has been about constantly grappling with achievement—striving to achieve. You have felt called to a purpose or a way to make a difference. Your work and your business have given you an extended community of people whom you proactively have chosen to work with and to share your life with. The work has given your life structure in terms of allocating your energy and your time.

During this first transition stage, it's important to recognize that you may temporarily lose much of this direction and structure. Before, your life was filled with lists of things to do, but now you may feel less urgency. As Roger Babson said, "The fun is in the striving, not the arriving." So what *is* the new sense of purpose or meaning that the post–wealth creation owner-manager strives for? How do you allocate your personal resources—your energy, time, capital, and passion—with as much urgency as you did 30 years ago in your business?

If you as owner-manager haven't thought through these questions in advance and haven't realized just what a huge change you are in for, you are likely to be caught off guard. You will be the same person you were before, but with different roles. Even though you will have achieved your dreamed-of long-term goals and earned a larger fortune than you ever imagined, you may feel a nagging sense of loss.

So during this first stage you work toward a new attitude and understanding of where you are. Entering the next chapter in your life is one of those rare life moments, such as moving out of your parents' home, going to or graduating from college, starting a job in a new industry, possibly exiting a failed relationship—where you get a chance to push the reset button, reinvent yourself, and decide what your new goals and purpose are really going to be.

You don't get many of these reset button chances in life, but this is one of them. And one great thing you can do is think deeply about behaviors that you now think of as bad habits—and work to change them. That doesn't mean you have to simply stop doing them. There's plenty of literature that explains why that approach doesn't work. But you can replace unproductive habits with new, productive ones.

You also have an opportunity to present yourself to new constituencies and to do so in an entirely new light. For example, you may think about and act on personal or social issues that matter to you and that you haven't been able to allocate the time to. As you increase your focus on generativity, you may reduce your focus on your own identity and achievement. You might think deeply about the relationships in your life—which ones are creating energy and which ones are draining it. This time offers you an unusual chance for glorious unsophistication and reinvention.

Two Who Had the Realization Early

Case in point: Mike and Joe. Awhile back, my partners and I met with them. As the meeting wrapped up, Mike and Joe looked across the table at my partners, David, Rob, and me. They co-owned a supersuccessful business in the branded food domain. "What we're looking for," Mike said, "is an M&A firm we can initiate a relationship with right now. We know we want to capture a gain someday, probably years from now. We're sure we will need a new majority investor with deep pockets who can fund our expansion, probably with a plant in Asia. We don't know what the best timing for that will be exactly. It could be next year; it could be three years from now. So we would like to begin thinking about meaningful changes we might make in the business to prepare for that. We're not talking about window dressing, but meaningful changes."

My partners and I looked at each other and grinned. "Wow," Rob said. "That is incredibly refreshing to hear. Usually we're the ones coaching our clients to slow down a bit, get their ducks in a row, and not dash into a transaction. It is so great to meet a prospective client who is already thinking that way."

"It's simple," said Joe. "I'm pretty sure what you're going to tell us. Since I have no intention of leading the business under new majority ownership, we have to have a management team ready to step up well before the transaction. We need to get the people and the plan in place now so that, professionally, I can exit upon the transaction. My wife and I intend to move our family from our home of the last 20 years in New York. We'll divide our time between our place on the coast of Maine and our cabin in the Rockies. I may or may not have another business start-up in me. It depends on if my kids want to start a business. If so, I'd back them. But we need to prepare for the new ownership right now. So, that's why we're talking with you. Where do we start?"

Stage 2: Hibernation

The second stage, the hibernation period, usually starts soon after the transaction. Hibernation is a natural dormant state resembling sleep, right? It's a kind of "resting up," in anticipation of the great activity that will come about in the spring. Many owner-managers coming through a 6- to 12-month professional transaction after 20 to 30 years of leading a private company *are* fatigued. Most of them have a lot of catching up to do in their personal lives. Many of my friends and clients go through a period of hibernation after the wealth creation event; they "sleep." You too will have time to reflect a bit on what was good and bad about your career experiences. You may think of some of the challenges and adversity you faced that built your strength and self-efficacy. You could reflect on what you would do differently if you were to do it all over again. What are some of the actions you would repeat? Which ones weren't so much fun; which would you try to avoid?

During the hibernation period, you may indeed sleep more and get up later than you have in a long time. This is a good time to catch up on the list of to-dos in your personal life. You may work out, sometimes more than once a day, and get in great physical shape. Some people keep a journal or a book of notes. One of my best friends scrawled his thoughts with colored markers on a wall-sized sheet of paper so he could see them all at once.

During this period, owner-managers usually come back to the idea that a clear purpose, fueled with passion, can result in an outcome they are proud of. They may also realize that a goal that is not passion-driven, but coupled only with skill, can feel more like an obligation than fun. They've had enough of those, and they usually avoid suggestions that they get involved in such activities.

In the hibernation phase, you don't want to be forced into making rapid decisions about your newly liquid wealth, your life activities, or . . . anything. It is a time of thinking and introspection mixed with feelings of loss, which can look a lot like mourning, although I don't think of it that way. I see it as a period of reflection and evaluation that is essential before you can return to purposeful work. You ask yourself about how to replace the energy, the fun, the sense of purpose, and the team you created around you in the previous chapter of your life. Sometimes, the owner-manager becomes an unintentional expert in social science, discovering that achieving great wealth doesn't result in subjective well-being . . . but unsure about what does.

And the questions just keep on coming: "What will I concentrate on? Which relationships formed during the period of building my business will last now that I have made the transition out? Now what are my philanthropic goals? Which institutions or projects should I fund? What is my philanthropic vision? Is it as clear as the vision I had for my business enterprise? How can I put my fortune to good use? How can I avoid squandering it—or standing by as my wealth advisors blow it for me? How will this newfound wealth and the additional time I have available change my relationship with my spouse and my kids? Will my kids be proud of me? Will my parents understand why this is good? How involved should I be in my own wealth management? After all, this will affect the lives of my wife, my kids, and even my grandkids."

Finally, you begin to think more deeply and philosophically about the nature of work itself and may even dip into the large body of scholarly literature on the topic. All successful owner-managers I know who go through this stage think about purpose, the challenge of building new relationships, the nature of how they want to invest their most precious resource, time—or as I like to think of it, positive energy—and, indeed, the benefits of work itself.

Busier Than Ever Doing Not Very Much

After Jeff did not reply to my third or fourth e-mail, I decided to call him on his cell. He picked up.

"How're you doin', buddy?" I asked. "I've been trying to reach you!"

"Oh, I know, Pete, I'm sorry," Jeff replied. "I haven't been good about checking my e-mail—doesn't seem like there's a helluva lot in it that's meaningful to me at the moment. Don't take it the wrong way. I am just preoccupied with getting caught up on some things on the home front. Marilyn says I am driving her nuts."

"Okay, but I've been trying to reach you about that advisory board I mentioned to you. I think you'd be a terrific candidate as a member. It's a business owned by a friend in the Pacific Northwest that manufactures parts for aircraft interiors. It is at about $110 million in revenues and solidly profitable. The owner is putting together his first advisory board, and given your experience in similar products for the automotive space, I thought of you. Plus, you'd really click with the owner, Bryce."

"Uh-huh," Jeff said noncommittally. "Well, is there something I can take a look at, some description of the company?"

"I gave you its website address, remember? Have you taken a look at that?"

"Oh, I think I lost that. Can you resend it? Sorry, Pete, we're just a little disorganized at the moment. I'm getting ready to be in a Half Ironman Triathlon in Arizona, and Marilyn is entering some of her watercolors in a show in Sedona at the same time. I know it doesn't sound like much, but we're busy, man. It's weird, but without the rigor of the day-to-day demands on me, it seems we're more busy than ever. I'll think some more about this business. Can I get back to you?"

Jeff, I could tell, was in deep hibernation mode. He was getting caught up with stuff in his personal life that he let go during the last couple years when he was managing the business that he just exited. He and Marilyn each had things they wanted to accomplish— some independently, some together. Before the transaction, Jeff had squeezed such things in around his more pressing, time-sequenced business objectives. In the posttransaction mode, he didn't have those clear objectives anymore (or, at least, not yet).

In hibernation mode it makes sense to get caught up. It seems very simple to just hang out, ignore the phone and the e-mail, and invest fully in some of the personal relationships and goals that may have been neglected due to the demands of the business.

189

But look out. Because we all know in nature what season comes after hibernation, right?

Stage 3: Experimentation

The third posttransaction phase is called the experimentation stage. In nature, what always comes after hibernation? Spring! The experimentation stage is like the reaction people have when spring comes after a long winter and they want to run outside and rip off all their clothes. Ta-da!

During this phase, owner-managers want to try things with their talent and with their wealth in a way they haven't pursued before. After hibernation they've had a realization that learning and growing are essential for them. They are probably thinking more about legacy and less about fortune. Frequently they want to get back in the game, but not in the same way or to the same extent they played it in earlier days: *Hibernation? Done that. Now I want to rock and roll.* Recall the character strengths of these people? They have hibernated, rested up, gotten in shape, and now—*click!*—it's springtime and they want to act.

They are driven to the experimentation phase by a growing feeling of unease with their hibernating habits. All that reflection and rumination and analysis paralysis! The unease grows into impatience, and they want to *get moving*, get on to the next thing. Enough of this confusing nowhere of in-betweenness. If they want to move but don't have a clear plan, they may become anxious, frantic, even desperate to act, to move on, to do something—anything—productive.

Mischief Can Happen

There is danger lurking in this phase. Because owner-managers are usually zestful, have attractive personalities, and are now highly liquid, they can quickly get into a lot of personal and professional mischief when that desire to move grows strong. Without taking into account issues of timing and luck, they naturally believe they can do again what they have already done so successfully. They may get the urge to provide seed funding to other start-up entrepreneurs, lending the glitter of their success to a new venture. This can work, but it can fail. A lot of newly realized wealth has been squandered on ventures that looked hot but turned out not to be.

This zeal for action is understandable, but most owner-managers forget that it took them two or three decades to build their company and create great wealth. As they try to get back in the flow, they feel keenly disadvantaged by the lack of structure and support they had created for themselves in their earlier enterprises. They feel great frustration that it takes longer to successfully get into action than they had expected. In my experience, *it can take years* to reach a point where you feel the flow again.

So Many Great Opportunities

My cell phone buzzed at 5:30 p.m. on a Sunday afternoon.

"Hey, Pete! I know you aren't in the business of evaluating investment opportunities, and I am keenly aware that I am not a paying client of yours any longer. But I was wondering if you could find time in your calendar to travel with me to Chicago this week. There's a very interesting medical company there, and I'm thinking of investing in it. It only needs about two million bucks to get FDA approval for the next stage of clinical trial. I could do that for them and go on their board too."

"Whoa! Whoa!" I said. "Who is this, anyway?" I was kidding; I knew exactly who it was. "Is this really Jana?" She assured me it was.

"Well," I said, "I have no particular knowledge in this rarified air of medical nanotechnology."

"I know, I know," Jana persisted. "But I really respect your opinion, and I'm in a hurry to put this capital in now before they contact anybody else. The president of the firm tells me that a number of experienced early-stage investors are clamoring to put in the capital, and I don't want to lose this opportunity."

"Whoa, again! Slow down." I said. "Are you the best possible investor for them, Jana? I mean, I loved what you did with the family industrial supply business: you created a ton of value for all the constituencies and brilliantly transitioned it to the strategic acquirer. But do you feel that you have unique abilities that apply in this medical space as well?"

"Good point, Pete," she said, slowing down a bit. "I don't want you to think this is the only investment I am evaluating. There's an interesting opportunity in a start-up software company in the B to B space, that's only about two hundred thousand. And I've been talking with my old college roommate about buying a catalogue business. She recently retired from L.L. Bean and knows a ton about catalogue sales."

"Jana," I persisted. "Let's talk a bit about the destination with this. Where are you trying to go with these investments? Are they passive investments that you hope to get a return on capital with, or are they situations that you bring value to as an engaged owner-manager?"

"Both," she replied. "I mean, I am definitely not willing to get back into the day-to-day muck of operations, but I might be willing to spend a couple of days a week helping out—I think I have a lot to offer, don't you?"

My inside voice whispers for Jana: *Danger. Danger.*

Stage 4: Reinvention

The fourth phase is the *reinvention stage*: reinvention of purpose, redefining what meaning will be for you; the reinvention of *striving* for purpose and meaning. During this stage the individual is searching for meaning, for moving beyond a concentration on the self to a focus on others. My definition of *meaning* is serving something that is bigger than you, that is timeless, that is beyond mere self-interest. For more insight on this, I refer you to the thought leadership on what Marty Seligman calls the Meaningful Life, or the Achieving Life in his book *Flourish* (2011).

The reinvention stage is often related to the legacy built in the owner-managed business. I have seen some owner-managers benefit by engaging in peer groups whose members come together to talk about issues of common interest: "How do I find a wealth advisor I can trust? How do I put my capital to use in a meaningful way? What do I want to achieve now and can I establish new relationships, networks, and talent to help me achieve it? Where can I find positive relationships with other people who are also energy creators, whom I can learn and grow from?"

One of the most important issues the owner-manager faces in this stage is how to achieve a new kind of balance in life. Most owner-managers don't want to be as completely absorbed in their new endeavors as they were in their businesses, because involvement could reach a level of preoccupation that many spouses and family members would call "neglect." There was little room in the family life for anything *but* the enterprise. But owner-managers do want to be back in the action and fully engaged in what they're doing. They want to experience the phenomenon that Mihalyi Csikszentmihalyi calls *flow* [in his book by the same term (1990)].

New, Very Different, Family Business

Have you taken a day off in the past nine months? George Gallagher hadn't. You'll recall George from Chapter 2: he deliberately carved out a role for himself as interim CEO of Gallagher Companies, when it was acquired by a prestigious private European strategic investor.

By then, George's extended family had transitioned from thinking about Gallagher as the family business to thinking about it as one of the assets that the family took care of together—and in that subtlety they found a world of difference. George and his immediate family—including his mother, his sister, and his sister's family—had all become involved in helping the homeless in the area where the Gallaghers lived. They especially wanted to help teens acquire skills that would enable them to find good employment and become independent. To that end, George and his family set up a charitable foundation and funded an apprenticeship program in the hospitality industry especially for homeless teens. There, they learned the basic skills of the trade and even operated a restaurant that's considered "hip" in its niche market.

George was surprised to find that running this not-for-profit operation took as much time, talent, and energy as running Gallagher Companies had. The Gallagher Family had found a new "family business."

An Unexpected Challenge: Wealth Management

There is another challenge awaiting you after the transaction event: the management of your newly liquid wealth. Although you have dealt with financial issues throughout your career, you, like many owner-managers, may not be particularly skilled at managing your own substantial wealth captured from the recapitalization or sale of the business. You discover that value creation is a very different endeavor than wealth management. And your natural distrust of outsiders and corporate types makes it hard for you to find a wealth management expert who by his behavior has earned your trust.

In your privately owned business, you knew exactly how to keep score: profit, usually measured in the form of EBITDA. Now your relationship with money is different. *What's the new scorecard?* You don't have to keep making more money. All you really need to do is preserve it. You'd like to see it grow, sure, but it's not the same as building sales, juggling cash flow, and optimizing your EBITDA. This presents a psychological challenge that some owner-managers respond to successfully but that others find difficult. Finding an advisor is tough enough. How the heck do you find advisors you can trust? How can you find friends you can learn and grow with? How do you know they're not just attracted by your wealth?

The hibernation stage is a good time to think about this matter and to build a financial plan to preserve the wealth you have worked so hard to gain. Doing so takes a major shift in thinking. Previously your goal was to build enterprise value; now your goal is to preserve the wealth that's sitting in the bank. The skill set that made you a successful owner-manager is different from the one needed to be a good investor in the public market. In fact, I would argue that the strengths that allowed you to be a great owner-manager are *opposite* to the characteristics of the good wealth manager in preservation mode. To paraphrase Daniel Kahneman, "Show me a successful entrepreneur and I will show you talent visited by luck. Show me a greatly successful entrepreneur and I will show you talent visited by great luck." Your wealth creation was generated through applying capital, talent, passion, and energy persistently—no, tirelessly— invested in an illiquid, risky, concentrated investment that had a 50 percent probability of failure in its first five years. You have personally had your fingers in the finger paint, and you have been good at it. In fact, the more you were a hands-on owner-manager, the more you accelerated the building of enterprise value.

Welcome to the new chapter. Professional wealth management requires you to allocate assets—in a coldly objective and patient way, disregarding all the noise around you—in a basket of assets that has some probability of earning the average market return and (one hopes) has little or no probability of blowing up.

It takes some time for most owner-managers to get their heads around this, and their investment objectives evolve during and after a wealth creation event. Many of them begin by not wanting to take any market risk, presumably because they have already taken enough market risk for one lifetime. And given the very large returns many of them earn in their private businesses, they are typically unimpressed by public market returns.

Over time, owner-managers may decide to take a degree of risk in order to preserve their purchasing power. Many come to the conclusion that it makes sense to maintain two accounts, each with a different goal. One is a no-risk portfolio; the other is assembled with the goal of achieving high returns and has the commensurate risk. The nonrisk portfolio contains the money you need to preserve to live and is invested so it cannot blow up. In that one, you are willing to trade off your return for safety. With the risky account, you're seeking a few concentrated investments that have high rates of return—similar to what you earned in your private business, and you accept the possibility of loss of capital in that account.

Preservation as a Goal: The Differences between Value Creation and Wealth Management

Just as owner-managers don't understand wealth management, many wealth managers are not clear about how posttransaction owner-managers feel about their investments. The wealth advisors will pepper you with questions about your "risk tolerance," snappily chatting away about modern portfolio theory and mean variance optimization, the optimum diversification strategy to result in the highest returns for you. But do they actually get the fact that you have made your fortune already? You aren't looking for them to make another fortune for you. You just want them to preserve the one you already earned—*the hard way.*

One of my good friends was shocked when he learned that the average return from the U.S. public equity market over the past 90 years was 9.8 percent per year. He also learned that "averages obscure." In fact, there were only 3 years of the past 90 that fell in the average zone (9 to 11 percent inclusive). Huh? Sure the average is 9.8 percent, but that average is made up of a scatter diagram of lots and lots of years that varied greatly from that mean. Apart from those three "average" years, the gains in most of the other years ranged from minus 10 percent to plus 20 percent.

Thinking about and being able to track performance in this way is very different from the way the owner-manager looks at gains in his business. In that situation, increases in enterprise value are discontinuous and aren't tracked anywhere; you can't check your Yahoo! page every minute to get a quote. The owner-manager learns the value of his enterprise only once in his entire career, which may span three decades or more. On the other side of the transaction, he becomes an obsessive portfolio watcher, which only has the effect of distracting him and turning him into an anxious, stressed-out loss avoider. What are the implications of this on the subjective well-being of the owner-manager? Of the portfolio?

The Unhappy Day Trader

To understand the problem of wealth management, let me paraphrase and repurpose a story originally related by Nassim Taleb (2001).

Let's say you are an owner-manager who recently had a successful wealth creation transaction. You're working with a wealth advisor who helps you to construct a great portfolio with a market return that is *way* above average—let's say 15 percent, with 10 percent variability. This means that 68 percent of the time your portfolio result will fall between the range of 5 to 25 percent.

Now let's suppose that you are in the hibernation phase. You have a lot of time on your hands and decide to follow your investments closely, which you have never done before. The probability you will make money in this portfolio over the course of a year is 93 percent—that is, if you check your account summary just once a year. If you check the bottom line once a quarter, however, the probability of making money drops to 77 percent. You're beginning to see "noise" not "signal." That's still pretty good, right? But that's not how you read it. You check that one-quarter loss and say, "Whoa! I lost some of my hard-earned money this quarter, what am I going to do?" And, of course, the pain gets worse the more often you check the portfolio, which can become an obsessive activity.

Because bad (a loss) feels so much stronger than good, the hibernating ex-owner-manager has to do something to relieve the pain. Our hero decides to become a trader. Since he has no experience at this, he often buys the wrong investments, at the wrong time, and sells the right investments, also at the wrong time. Pretty soon, the portfolio is a mess.

It may seem paradoxical that the active involvement of the owner-manager in his business creates wealth, but active involvement in the investment portfolio may destroy it. I cannot think of a single owner-manager who acts as his own wealth manager after the acquisition of his company who is having fun, creating positive energy, and being as successful as he would like to be.

Personal Disruption of the Professional Transaction

Let me conclude by observing (and I say this with great affection): no matter how experienced, successful, and smart you are as an

owner-manager, you will be surprised at how diffi
from business owner to former business owner wil

My owner-manager friends and clients almos
timate the disruption and dislocation sparked b
wealth creation transaction. They may begin the p
the next majority owner of their business (the pro
tion) without thinking about and analyzing the sk
can bring them into new endeavors (personal trans
many of them are vulnerable to feelings of disori
do I go on Monday morning?"), loss, sadness, and
ing new purposeful work. They are often so dis
them years to develop the next really rewarding cha

Almost all my owner-manager friends and client
it to be a challenge, and a source of giant anxiet
advisors who are active listeners and who empathize
tion. Moving from concentrated illiquid, risky, han
ation to becoming a passive investor who entrusts fi
to advisors is more than challenging; it is fundame
for these characters.

Now, if, like me, you've had it with *reading* abo
capture, and savor enterprise value and now want
do about it, you are there. In the brief conclusion th
want to suggest a few things to keep in mind if yo
successful owner-manager and intend to have a capit
It's called The Beginning.

7

The Beginning of the Legacy

THIS BRIEF BOOK CONCLUDES WITH TWO METATHOUGHTS. THE first is tactical and the second is philosophical.

I'll start with the tactical. If you want to have a capital gain and a positive legacy *someday*, what are the half dozen actions you should take *right now*?

1. *Personal transition*. Begin by asking yourself, "What are my (and my spouse's or family's) personal goals? How does achieving a capital gain transaction get us closer to them? Do I know what my purpose and my mission are? Do I know what I will be striving for in the next chapter of my life after there is a new majority owner for my business?" If you don't identify the destination clearly, then it's not possible to put together an intelligent road map.

2. *Strategy*. Ask yourself, "Is my business in an industry that allows a capital gain? If so, is its strategy sufficiently clear and simple that I can articulate it in one sentence—even better, that the *customers* can repeat it in one sentence? Is my strategy such that it will build the business for the long, long [100-year] term? Is

what we are delivering to customers of such immense value that it will result in superior profits to our firm? Is my industry in or out of favor with institutional investors? Is our strategy so clear that we are disciplined to say 'no' to business that is not a great strategic fit?"

3. *Management team.* Ask yourself, "Do I have the management team in place that the next investor will require? Am I willing to make myself vulnerable by having my team know my personal goals? Have I informed my team of my interest in a capital gain someday, and have I aligned their compensation generally with that? Do I have the courage to make the changes necessary in the team so that we have the capacity to manage a business that is double our current size? Do we use the vocabulary of enterprise value?"

4. *Team of advisors.* Ask yourself, "Have I assembled the best possible world-class team of advisors who will help me achieve my personal and professional goals through capturing a capital gain? Am I willing to deliberately and generously push beyond my historic legacy advisors who have served me well but who may not be the ones to take me to the Promised Land? Am I willing to confide in this team of advisors (an attorney, accountant, M&A advisor, wealth advisor, board member, psychologist, and others) about what my future goals are? Am I ready to listen to and pay for potentially 'tough love' as professional advice?"

5. *Metrics.* Ask yourself, "Are my management team and I measuring the performance of the business the same way that coldly objective outsider investors will? Am I identifying and employing metrics that allow me to measure the drivers of value in my industry so I can measure if I am making progress on building enterprise value as an owner, by the day-to-day decisions I am making as a manager?"

6. *Legacy*. Ask yourself, "With all stakeholders, am I behaving in a way—and causing my organization to behave in a way—that my family and I are proud of? Am I (and my team) acting with passion and persistence for our long-term goals?"

Now for the philosophy.

Perhaps you have heard the name Dodge Morgan. He was a fiercely independent, salty, positive, confident, generous, and demanding character filled with zest. As an iconic entrepreneur owner-manager, he was completely immersed in building and capturing private company enterprise value, and aware that he was creating legacy on the way. He successfully turned around a failing company called Controlonics in the 1970s. And with the support of some wise mentors and contributions from a loyal, patient, and skilled management team, he built its enterprise value through technical tinkering. Ultimately he captured its millions of dollars of value in a sale to a strategic acquirer in the early 1980s.

Morgan made his professional transition quite smoothly, mostly because he was called to the next chapter and knew what it would involve. At age 54, after he made the transition, he became the first American to sail solo nonstop around the world, breaking the standing world record—in fact, cutting it in half. Throughout that 150-day journey aboard his Ted Hood–designed, purpose-built vessel, *American Promise*, Morgan was utterly alone, never touched land, and did not once use the engine.

To the media and to the casual observer, Morgan's journey might seem to have been compressed into just two days: the November day he anxiously departed St. George's Harbor in Bermuda and the day he returned there the following April, looking tanned and triumphant. What no one witnessed was everything in between, and there was a lot of it: the 30 days he spent slatting through windless calms, his loneliness and exhaustion and fear, the failure of critical equipment, the times he had to climb the eight-story mast to make repairs, weathering the 70-mph winds of a three-day tropical storm—all of this action was caught on film and eventually became a PBS documentary. One of my favorite moments in the film came when Morgan caught sight of the first tourist boat welcoming him back to Bermuda and exclaimed to himself, "Dammit, Dodge, you did it. You *did* it Dodge. Dammit, you did it!"

Another memorable moment came when the sea was calm and the video camera caught Morgan, below decks, talking to himself philosophically. "How do I feel?" he asked. "Lonely. I miss my wife. I miss my kids. I am so lucky to have them. Why did I decide to do this? I have a perfectly good normal life, I didn't have to do this, to come out here all on my own?"[1]

And then he went on deck, noticed that the breeze had gone aft, cracked the sheets, and urged himself on to his next immediate goal: rounding Cape Horn. At that moment Dodge epitomized the character strengths of an owner-manager: authenticity, gratitude, zest, but most of all, *grit*. He had the passion and persistence needed to set and realize long-term goals.

Toward the end of his life, however, Morgan said that he didn't consider his solo round-the-world voyage to be his greatest accomplishment. No, it was the things he had built with others: recruiting and working with his team to build the company; choosing Ted Hood and working with a small group of talented designers and artisans to build his cutter, *American Promise*; raising a family. His pride in his solo accomplishments was illuminated by his long relationships he was most proud of—the way he and his team ran it, the value it generated, and, most of all, the contributions he and his management team were able to make to its long-term success.

This is frequently true for most owner-managers. No matter what fabulous things they do in the chapters that follow a transaction, the most important part of the story is still that of the enterprise and the meaning it had for everyone involved.

First comes the meaning to the individual. As an owner-manager you have devoted the better part of your life and energy to building the business. You want the company to continue after your involvement is over and in the way you would prefer. Most owner-managers do not want to see their companies disappear or managed in directions they can't support.

To be completely fulfilled, these wild beasts affectionately called owner-managers have to understand this: the natural human condition is to tirelessly strive—and yet never really arrive at a "place called fulfillment." Striving is a behavior that humans have inherited over thousands of years of biological selection, and it is imprinted in our DNA. It's what we—especially entrepreneur owner-managers—are built to do. If we can understand that our striving can result in learning and growing and never-ending positive change, then with that wisdom we *are* in a completely fulfilled place.

Second, the transaction has tremendous implications for the family members and their future, what they can and will do, and how they will relate to each other. They too will go through stages not dissimilar to those experienced by owner-managers.

Some family stakeholders think of "the family business" rather than as "one of the assets the family owns." There's a world of difference between the two attitudes. Family businesses are prone to be internally focused. The company can become distracted by relationships among family members. It can also get into an unhealthy area when management succession becomes an issue, especially when it is a "given" that the successor CEO will be a family member—regardless of that person's ability, desire, or even willingness to serve in that capacity. That's "family business thinking."

Thinking of the business as "one of the assets our family owns together," on the other hand, usually means that family members are able to come together and make more objective decisions about the health of the business, the allocation of finite resources, management performance, the need for liquidity, and much more. Through this lens, individuals in the family can separate their roles as family members from their roles as managers in the business (if, in fact, they play a role in the company). Then, when it is time to seek a new CEO or other key leader, they can make the choice based on qualifications and fit rather than by possession of a family name or the dictates of tradition.

Finally, although as an owner-manager you are focused on the impact of the transaction on yourself and your family, and you're concerned with the company's future, the transaction can also affect a broader set of stakeholders, an extended community, and even our society as a whole.

Let me explain.

The Greater Contribution

The likelihood that an owner-manager like you will achieve a capital gain so great as to impress others as mind-blowing is logically supportable if you measure the risks all owner-managers and their investors (both winners and losers) take as a group. Common sense says that if there were not the potential for a great return, very few intelligent people would play the game, one in which they must "bet the farm" and in which the odds of winning are 50-50. To make the risk acceptable, therefore, the potential gain to the owner-manager must be extraordinary—greatly outsized in comparison to other investment gains. The potential gain must be enormous not only to reward the owner-manager for this undertaking but also to create a "return on investment" for *all* the owner-managers who make attempts, including those who fail to make a gain.

It is sensible, therefore, that the gains of any one successful owner-manager should not be measured simply against the capital and effort at risk in his or her *specific* enterprise. Instead, it should be measured against the effort and capital at risk of *all* entrepreneurs, including the 50 percent I don't focus on in this book—those who made attempts and lost. And many have failed. Most of those who do fail go on to some other kind of work, but some of them try again, manage to forge a new business on the embers of loss, and succeed. I salute them.

But the brilliance of entrepreneurial capitalism, it seems to me, is that this system allows seemingly self-centered goals at an *individual* level to be transformed into highly beneficial outcomes for our society as a whole.

Take a look at the following list of 10 names. Do you recognize the names and understand why I have ranked them in this order?

Gates
Ford
Getty
Johnson
Hewlett
Kellogg
Lilly
Packard
MacArthur
Moore

Yes, these people are great examples of entrepreneur owner-managers. Each one of these people earned his wealth through building and capturing the value of his company. (Bill Gates/ Microsoft; Henry Ford/Ford Motor Company; J. Paul Getty/Getty Oil Company; the Johnson brothers/Johnson & Johnson; Bill Hewlett/Hewlett-Packard; Will Keith Kellogg/Kellogg Company; Eli Lilly/Eli Lilly & Co.; David Packard/Hewlett-Packard; John D. MacArthur/Bankers Life & Casualty; Charles Moore/Intel Corporation.)

But these entrepreneurs are, or were, also something much more than business owners and managers. Ranked in this order, these are the names of the *top 10 charitable foundations in the United States ranked by the market value of their assets*, based on the most current audited financial data[2] as of March 2013. These foundations are the top funders of the not-for-profit social sector in the United States.

Notice there is no Jack Welch Foundation on the top 10, nor is there a John Hammergren, Meg Whitman, or Carly Fiorina foundation. I am not casting any aspersions on any of these well-known CEOs, all of whom have appeared on the *Forbes* list of Top Ten CEOs in America. But they do not appear in the top 10 charitable foundations because they were employees of their companies, not the owner-managers. They were agents for the owners, not principals for their own account. They earned good salaries, but they did not create the truly sustainable wealth or legacy that can only be achieved by building and capturing value in an enterprise you manage.

I have written this book for entrepreneur owner-managers, the most proeconomic, prosocial people on the planet. To you—the entrepreneur owner-managers, the wealth builders, the creators of huge value for themselves and for their society—I say: thank you and good luck. I wish you an energizing and memorable journey and, to paraphrase the words of Sting, in every step you take, I'll be watching you, as you strive, grow, succeed, and achieve the legacy that you've worked so hard to build.

Notes

Introduction

1. Kauffmann, 2010.

Chapter 1

1. American Psychologist, January 2000; Volume 55 No. 1—"Positive Psychology: An Introduction," Martin E.P. Seligman and Mihaly Csikszentmihalyi, pp. 5–14.
2. VIA Institute on Character. "The VIA® Classification of Character Strengths." Last modified April 2013. http://www.viacharacter.org/www/en-us/viainstitute/classification.aspx.
3. Bigelow. "Loss Aversion." Last modified April 24, 2013. http://bigelowllc.com/PDFs/messages/Loss%20Aversion.pdf.
4. Bigelow. "Endowment Bias." Last modified April 2013. http://www.bigelowllc.com/PDFs/messages/Endowment%20Bias.pdf.

Chapter 6

1. Peter Worrell. "Fighting with One's Self," Positive Psychology. Last modified August 17, 2011. http://positivepsychologynews.com/news/peter-worrell/2011081718907.
2. Worrell. "Fighting with One's Self."

Chapter 7

1. *Around Alone*, DVD (1987; Cambridge, MA: The New Film Company, Inc., 1997).
2. Foundation Center. "Top 100 U.S. Foundations by Asset Size." Last modified December 31, 2011. http://foundationcenter.org/findfunders/topfunders/top100assets.html.

A Note on Sources
and Bibliography

OVER THE PAST 30 YEARS THERE HAS BEEN A REVOLUTION—MAYBE it's more precise to call it a rebellion—in the cognitive sciences. Not long ago, the application of the theoretical fundamentals of a specific discipline was largely confined to the academic silo. Transdisciplinary sharing of knowledge was not encouraged, and it was often regarded with suspicion. Over the past three decades, however, a constellation of gifted thinkers has observed and written about the patterns of knowledge that integrate seemingly unrelated disciplines. These academics have enlightened us and created a great deal of energy around their ideas. Their insights in the areas of finance and psychology particularly relate to my work with entrepreneur owner-managers.

I believe the great breakthroughs over the *next* 30 years will not be related to technology or social media or any other particular pursuit of current interest but rather will emerge as the result of the consilience of knowledge that transcends disciplines. Here are two simple examples.

Daniel Kahneman and Amos Tversky, two Israeli-American psychologists, worked together over a period of many years, conducting research into a number of topics, including decision making. One of their important observations was that, when making important decisions, people often acted irrationally—that is, not in their own logical self-interest. Kahneman and Tversky theorized that this was because their subjects used mental shortcuts, or rules of thumb, that saved mental processing time but often produced less-than-optimal results. The researchers termed these "heuristics." The two, along with many others, soon saw that their ideas were not only transportable to other academic disciplines but were also applicable to economics and finance, particularly business decision making and the domain of risk. (Kahneman was the first psychologist to receive the Nobel Prize in Economic Sciences, in 2002.)

Martin Seligman and Mihaly Csikszentmihalyi are the cofounders of the field of positive psychology. Positive psychology combines theory, research, and applications to achieve an understanding of the positive aspects of human behavior that lead to a life of thriving or flourishing. Positive psychology is intended to supplement, not replace, traditional psychology. Csikszentmihalyi was a psychology researcher intensely interested in intrinsic motivation, optimal performance, and what came to be known as "flow," a feeling of being totally engaged or absorbed in the task at hand, resulting in feelings of great fulfillment, elevation, and happiness. Seligman, a highly regarded academic as well as a hands-on clinical psychologist, observed that the characteristics that allowed his patients to recover from clinically identifiable illnesses were not the same characteristics that needed to be strengthened in order to perform at optimal levels. This "jumping together," or consilience, of seemingly unrelated research resulted in the founding of a whole new field.

The work of Kahneman has jumped together with that of Seligman and Csikszentmihalyi, and Kahneman has become an important thought leader in positive psychology. He writes about the "experiencing self" in contrast to the "remembering self," and also on peak-end theory, wealth, life satisfaction, and more. All of these issues pertain to the work and nature of the entrepreneur owner-manager.

The following are some of the books that have shaped my thinking and that I recommend for further reading.

Akerlof, George K., and Robert J. Shiller. *Animal Spirits: How Human Psychology Drives the Economy, and Why It Matters for Global Capitalism*. Princeton: Princeton University Press, 2009.

Babson, Roger W. *Actions and Reactions: An Autobiography of Roger W. Babson*. New York: Harper and Brothers, 1935.

Barzun, Jacques. *The House of Intellect*. New York: Harper and Brothers, 1959.

Bell, Daniel. *The Cultural Contradictions of Capitalism*. Cambridge, MA: Perseus Publishing, 1976.

Bernstein, Peter L. *Against the Gods: The Remarkable Story of Risk*. New York: Wiley, 1996.

Bogle, John C. *Enough: True Measures of Money, Business and Life*. Hoboken, NJ: Wiley, 2009.

Brooks, David. *The Social Animal: The Hidden Sources of Love, Character and Achievement*. New York: Random House, 2011.

Brown, Brene. *Daring Greatly*. New York: Gotham Books, 2012.

Butman, John. *Breaking Out*. Boston: Harvard Business Review Press, 2013.

Christensen, Clayton M. *How Will You Measure Your Life?* New York: Harper Business, 2012.

Cialdini, Robert B. *Influence: The Psychology of Persuasion*. New York: Quill, 1984.

Crawford, Matthew B. *Shop Class as Soul Craft: An Inquiry into the Value of Work*. New York: Penguin, 2009.

Csikszentmihalyi, Mihaly. *Flow: The Psychology of Optimal Experience*. New York: Harper, 1990.

Darwin, Charles. *Voyage of the Beagle*. New York: Penguin, 1989 (1839).

Defoe, Daniel. *Robinson Crusoe*. New York: World Syndicate Publishing Company, 1932.

Duhigg, Charles. *The Power of Habit: Why We Do What We Do in Life and Business*. New York: Random House, 2012.

Ellis, Charles D. *Investment Policy: How to Win the Losers Game*. Homewood, IL: Dow Jones-Irwin, 1985.

Elster, John. *Explaining Social Behavior: More Nuts and Bolts for the Social Sciences*. Cambridge, UK: Cambridge University Press, 2007.

Erricson, K. Anders. *The Influence of Experience and Deliberate Practice on the Development of Superior Expert Performance*. Cambridge, UK: Cambridge University Press, 2006.

Feynman, Richard P. *The Pleasure of Finding Things Out*. Cambridge, MA: Perseus Publishing, 1999.

Franco, Carol, and Kent Linebach. *The Legacy Guide*. New York: Tarcher Penguin, 2006.

Fredrickson, Barbara L. *Positivity*. New York: Crown Publishers, 2009.

Gawande, Atul. *Better: Surgeons Notes on Performance*. New York: Picador, 2007.

Gilbert, Daniel. *Stumbling on Happiness*. New York: Alfred A. Knopf, 2007.

Grant, Adam. *Give and Take: A Revolutionary Approach to Success*. New York: Viking, 2013.

Haidt, Jonathan. *The Righteous Mind: Why Good People Are Divided by Politics and Religion*. New York: Pantheon, 2012.

Harford, Tim. *Why Success Always Starts with Failure*. New York: Farrar, Strauss and Giroux, 2011.

Jamison, Kay Redfield. *Exuberance: The Passion for Life.* New York: Alfred A. Knopf, 2004.

Kahneman, Daniel. *Thinking Fast and Slow.* New York: Farrar, Strauss and Giroux, 2011.

Kahneman, Daniel, Paul Slovic, and Amos Tversky. *Judgment under Uncertainty: Heuristics and Biases.* Cambridge, UK: Cambridge University Press, 1982.

Kahneman, Daniel, and Amos Tversky. *Choices, Values, and Frames.* Cambridge, UK: Cambridge University Press, 2000.

Konner, Melvin. *Why the Reckless Survive: And Other Secrets of Human Nature.* New York: Viking Press, 1990.

Lowenstein, Roger. *When Genius Failed: The Rise and Fall of Long-Term Capital Management.* New York: Random House, 2000.

Marks, Howard. *The Most Important Thing Illuminated: Uncommon Sense for the Thoughtful Investor.* New York: Columbia University Press, 2013.

Mauboussin, Michael J. *More Than You Know: Finding Financial Wisdom in Unconventional Places.* New York: Columbia University Press, 2006.

———. *The Success Equation: Untangling Skill and Luck in Business, Sports, and Investing.* Boston: Harvard Business Review Press, 2012.

———. *Think Twice: Harnessing the Power of Counter Intuition.* Boston: Harvard Business Press, 2009.

McCraw, Thomas K. *Prophet of Innovation: Joseph Schumpeter and Creative Destruction.* Cambridge, MA: Harvard University Press, 2007.

Meadows, Donella H. *Thinking in Systems.* White River Junction, VT: Chelsea Green Publishing Company, 2008.

Mlodinow, Leonard. *Subliminal: How Your Unconscious Mind Rules Your Behavior.* New York: Pantheon, 2012.

Montier, James. *Behavioural Investing: A Practitioners Guide to Applying Behavioral Finance.* West Sussex, England: Wiley Finance, 2007.

Morgan, Dodge. *Voyage of American Promise.* New York: Houghton Mifflin, 1989.

Murray, Charles. *Coming Apart: The State of White America, 1960–2010.* New York: Random House, 2012.

Nassar, Sylvia. *Grand Pursuit: The Story of Economic Genius.* New York: Simon and Schuster, 2011.

Nomura, Catherine, and Julia Waller. *Unique Ability: Creating the Life You Want.* Toronto: Strategic Coach, 2003.

Pallotta, Dan. *Uncharitable: How Restraints on Nonprofits Undermine Their Potential.* Medford, MA: Tufts University Press, 2008.

Peterson, Christopher. *Pursuing the Good Life.* Oxford, UK: Oxford University Press, 2013.

Peterson, Christopher, and Martin E. P. Seligman. *Character Strengths and Virtues: A Handbook and Classification.* Oxford, UK: Oxford University Press, 2004.

Pink, Daniel H. *To Sell Is Human: The Surprising Truth About Moving Others.* New York: Riverhead Books, 2012.

Pinker, Steven. *How the Mind Works.* New York: W.W. Norton, 1997.

Popper, Karl. *The Logic of Scientific Discovery.* London: Routledge, 2002.

Poundstone, William. *Prisoner's Dilemma.* New York: Random House, 1992.

Posner, Richard A. *A Failure of Capitalism: The Crisis of '08 and the Descent into Depression.* Cambridge, UK: Harvard University Press, 2009.

Rath, Tom. *Strengths Finder 2.0.* New York: Gallup Press, 2007.

Ratey, John J. *Spark: The Revolutionary New Science of Exercise and the Brain.* New York: Little, Brown and Company, 2008.

Reivich, Karen, and Andrew Shatte. *The Resilience Factor: Seven Keys to Finding Your Inner Strengths and Overcoming Life's Hurdles.* New York: Broadway Books, 2002.

Ridley, Matt. *The Rational Optimist: How Prosperity Evolves.* New York: HarperCollins, 2010.

Rollnick, Stephen, and William R. Miller. *Motivational Interviewing: Preparing People for Change.* New York: Guilford Press, 2002.

Rosenstein, Bruce. *Living In More Than One World: How Peter Drucker's Wisdom Can Inspire and Transform Your Life.* San Francisco: Barrett Koehler Publishers, 2009.

Samuelson, William and Richard Zeckhauser. "Status Quo Bias in Decision Making," *Journal of Risk and Uncertainty*, 1:7–59, 1988.

Schwartz, Barry. *The Paradox of Choice: Why More Is Less.* New York: HarperCollins, 2004.

Seligman, Martin E. P. *Authentic Happiness: Using Positive Psychology to Realize Your Potential for Lasting Fulfillment.* New York: Free Press, 2002.

———. *Flourish: A Visionary New Understanding of Happiness and Well-Being.* New York: Free Press, 2011.

Seligman, Martin E. P., and Mihalyi Csikszentmihalyi. *Positive Psychology: An Introduction.* Washington, DC: American Psychological Association, 2000.

Siegel, Eric. *Predictive Analytics: The Power to Predict Who Will Click, Buy, Like, or Die.* Hoboken, NJ: Wiley, 2013.

Silver, Nate. *The Signal and the Noise: Why So Many Predictions Fail—But Some Do Not.* New York: Penguin, 2012.

Simon, Herbert A. *Models of My Life.* New York: HarperCollins, 1991.

Smith, Earl L. *Yankee Genius: A Biography of Roger W. Babson*. New York: Harper and Brothers, 1954.

Taleb, Nassim. *Fooled by Randomness: The Hidden Role of Chance in the Markets and Life*. New York: Texere, 2001.

———. *The Black Swan: The Impact of the Highly Improbable*. New York: Random House, 2007.

———. *Anti-Fragile: Things That Gain from Disorder*. New York: Random House, 2012.

Thaler, Richard H. *Advances in Behavioral Finance*. Princeton: Princeton University Press, 1993.

———. *Advances in Behavioral Finance II*. Princeton: Princeton University Press, 2005.

———. *The Winners Curse: Paradoxes and Anomalies of Economic Life*. Princeton: Princeton University Press, 1992.

———. "Toward a Positive Theory of Consumer Choice," *Journal of Economic Behavior and Organization*, 1:39–60, 1980.

Thaler, Richard H., and Cass R. Sunstein. *Nudge: Improving Decisions about Health, Wealth and Happiness*. New York: Caravan, 2008.

Uglow, Jenny. *The Lunar Men: Five Friends Whose Curiosity Changed the World*. New York: Farrar, Strauss and Giroux, 2002.

von Neumann, John, and Oskar Morgenstern. *Theory of Games and Economic Behavior*. Princeton: Princeton University Press, 1944.

Wilson, Edward O. *Consilience: The Unity of Knowledge*. New York: Random House, 1998.

———. *The Social Conquest of Earth*. New York: W.W. Norton, 2012.

Zeckhauser, Bryn, and Aaron Sandoski. *How the Wise Decide*. New York: Crown Business, 2008.

Zeckhauser, Richard J., and John W. Pratt. *Principles and Agents: An Overview*. Cambridge, MA: Harvard Business School Press, 1986.

Index

Note: Boldface numbers indicate illustrations

About the Author

Peter R. Worrell is the CEO and Managing Director of Bigelow LLC, which has been his professional home since 1980. Bigelow is an independent M&A advisory boutique, nationally known for being exclusively dedicated to clients that are private entrepreneur owner-managed businesses.

He has focused a significant portion of his professional life working at the intersection of psychology and finance, employing real-world, practical applications of insights from those disciplines to improve owner-manager decision making. He has authored or coauthored research on the character strengths of entrepreneurs and the risk tolerance of entrepreneurs.

Worrell is one of only a few hundred people in the country to have an advanced degree in Positive Psychology (MAPP-PENN). He has been awarded an Honorary Doctorate from Saint Michaels College. He and his spouse are cruising sailors who have left their wake on many of the world's oceans so far.